BETTY GROFF COOKBOOK

Pennsylvania German Recipes

Betty Groff Cookbook
Pennsylvania German Recipes
Recipes and text © 2001 by Betty Groff
Photography © 2001 by Blair Seitz
ISBN 1-879441-84-5

LOC Control # 2001 132084

Seitz & Seitz, Inc.
1010 North Third Street
Harrisburg, PA 17102
www.celebratePA.com

Designed by Klinginsmith & Company

Printed in China by Regent Publishing Services
St. Louis, MO 63123

*Amish children drop seedlings into cultivated rows
as an older boy drives the mules. Previous Page:
Lancaster County's rich soil yields bountiful crops.*

BETTY GROFF COOKBOOK

Pennsylvania German Recipes

Published by

RB
BOOKS
Harrisburg, PA

Betty Groff *as told to*
Diane Stoneback
Photography by Blair Seitz

TABLE OF CONTENTS

DANDELION SALAD WITH
HOT BACON DRESSING
Page 26

BRISKET OF BEEF
Page 55

EGG CHEESE
Page 89

APRICOT-NUT BREAD
Page 101

STRAWBERRY SHORTCAKE
Page 121

FUNNEL CAKES
Page 136

INTRODUCTION

The past is never far from the present in Lancaster County, the heart of Pennsylvania Dutch country. Just venture along our back roads and you'll experience sights, sounds, and even tastes of earlier times.

An Amish farmer guides a team of muscular workhorses straining to plow his fields for spring planting...Dresses, shirts, and trousers in somber black, gray, blue, green, and purple hues air-dry on a backyard clothesline, snapping and flapping, flag-like in the wind...The bell of a one-room schoolhouse still rings to summon children in from playing tag, seesawing, and swinging until their toes touch the sky...Sleek carriage horses pull trim black buggies into a farmyard where they're unhitched and tethered to wait until their owners finish attending church in a neighbor's home...Windmills standing next to whitewashed barns harness the breeze to power a world where electricity, automobiles, and other worldly goods are spurned. These magnificent scenes are framed by a patchwork of green fields, lush gardens, and fruitful orchards so productive that they've earned the county's residents a reputation for good farming and good food.

The Amish, the Mennonites (including my family), and many of the "English" (the Amish term for everyone else) never have had to get back to basics because they never abandoned them. The people here always have focused on the fruits and vegetables that are in season, have kept to simple but flavorful food preparations, and know the little culinary tricks that can make good ingredients taste even better.

Planning, planting, picking, and preserving the abundance that emerged from the land were my family's goals, just as they were at neighbor-

Right: As they did in my youth, the plain people of Lancaster County store canned fruits and vegetables in their cellars.

ing Amish farms. Although our families used different farming methods, the end results were fruits and vegetables with as much sparkle and beauty as gems in a jewelry store.

In addition to the foods we grew, the land generously provided us with a plateful of wild ingredients. We gathered shellbarks (similar to hickory nuts), plucked black raspberries from tangled and sharply pointed canes, harvested spindly but flavorful spears of wild asparagus, used cloves of wild garlic, and even coveted the weed that almost everyone loves to hate—the dandelion.

While the rest of the nation's cooks dabbled first with French, Italian, Mexican, and Chinese cuisines and then moved on to more exotic cuisines like those of India, Africa, and the Middle and Far East, we have never lost sight of our own culinary roots.

When America's regional cuisines such as Cajun, California, and Tex-Mex seized people's imaginations, we waited patiently for ours to be discovered. When cooks were on the edge of the Pacific Rim and dabbling in ethnic blends to create Mexican spaghetti and Peking duck tacos, we figured Pennsylvania's time would come.

But the potential of our Pennsylvania Dutch cuisine has been hampered by the often-over-played characterization of heavy meals focused solely on meat and potatoes and ever-followed by slices of super-sweet shoofly pie.

Lancaster County cooks' mastery of "one-pot" meals before the term was coined and their penchant for preparing meatless meals before vegetarianism came into vogue have been overlooked. Few realize Pennsylvania cooks were making all kinds of shaped pastas (we called them "noodles") before the Mediterranean diet sailed around the world. And although few people have noticed, we also have learned our share for modifying recipes or techniques to keep the country flavor in the hearty meals we serve.

Now, as basic foods such as macaroni and cheese, mashed potatoes, and rice pudding are being rediscovered, and as harried home cooks look for simple ways to get meals on their tables, I invite you to try my recipes drawn from the comfort foods I remember and cherish.

--Betty Groff

Top Left: Today, one-room schoolhouses similar to those I attended are located on Amish farms. Above: The farms of Lancaster County, Pennsylvania, my childhood home, are richly productive.

GARDEN

*F*lower gardens and fields are to spring and summer what quilts are to autumn and winter—the fabric that conveys the color of Lancaster County.

Lettuce, spinach, spring onions, asparagus, sugar peas, dandelion and watercress are the first shades of green on the springtime palette, along with strawberry-, rhubarb- and radish-reds, the brilliant orange of baby carrots, and the muted browns of walnut-sized new potatoes. As the growing season progresses, dramatic additions of color and flavor come from red and yellow tomatoes, a rainbow's worth of sweet peppers, dark purple eggplant, yellow and white sweet corn, cucumbers, string beans, assorted squash, and pumpkins.

But the groundwork for this bountiful season begins months in advance of the warm weather. I don't think my parents enjoyed anything much more than settling into easy chairs and paging through the new seed catalogs that arrived at nearly the same time as some of our worst winter snowstorms. Studying the drawings, pictures, and descriptions of juicy tomatoes, dark red

Left: Garden produce is bountiful and available in the many markets in Lancaster County.

beets, and snappy green beans seemed to rejuvenate us when the winds howled around the house and the outdoor water pump's trough still glistened under thick layers of ice.

My turn to read the catalogs came in the evening, after I'd been skating or sledding outdoors, had finished my homework, and was ready for bed. I loved the bright colors and descriptions of gardeners' successes. I had my own list of favorites, however, based on good taste plus the extra portion of fun they provided.

There were the vines of late-maturing pole beans that poked and twisted their way in and out of tall, three-sided wooden frames to

become a children's village of teepees. During games of hide 'n' seek with my brother and cousins, or even during hot days when I had a little time to spare, I scrambled to take cover in these garden hideaways.

Equally enjoyable were thoughts of the aroma and sounds of our garden-grown pop- corn exploding as we took turns shaking it in a wire basket with a long wooden handle on the coal stove.

But watermelons came the closest to being my idea of the world's most perfect crop. A half-moon-shaped slice, cut from a melon chilling in a galvanized tub of icy water, said "Summer"

with every bite. We loved the fruit, and even looked forward to the sweet, crunchy "watermelon" pickles my mother and aunt made by cutting the green rinds into thin strips. But there was more to savor, beyond the watermelons' food value. Their seeds provided us with a summer's worth of seed-spitting contests.

After the catalogs had been scanned to select the varieties our family would plant, the adults carefully calculated the quantities of seeds and plants they'd need to fill the kitchen garden and, ultimately, the dinner tables and pantries both uphome (in my parents' house at the top of the hill) as well as downhome (where my grandparents, aunt and uncle, and their children lived). It was certainly no small order because there were 12 people in the family, to say nothing of the hired hands and visitors who joined us at the table.

Enough corn would be ordered to provide us with corn-on-the-cob at every meal for the entire growing season. We were determined to enjoy it while it lasted, because produce was much more seasonal in those days before the entire world became our vegetable garden.

Ample tomatoes would be selected for slicing in salads and sandwiches as well as for "putting up" (canning) as tomato juice and sauce. Old standards and some new varieties, always promising the most flesh and fewest seeds, were tops on the list. An additional six plants yielding "exotic" yellow tomatoes also would go into the ground because the fruits were milder, less acidic, and made for more colorful arrangements on platters. In all, we'd order enough tomato seeds to fill two rows, with each containing 24 plants spaced 24 inches apart.

Previous Pages: Lancaster's plain people frequently border their gardens with an array of flowers. Right: In a scene reminiscent of my childhood, youths harvest potatoes on a Mennonite farm.

We sorted through the seed potatoes that would be cut into chunks, with each chunk containing an eye that would become a new plant. We took a count and ordered extra onion sets if enough baby bulbs hadn't been saved from the previous year's harvest.

By the time icicles started losing their grip on the rain gutters and thudding to the ground, the farms were coming back to life. The men were in the barns, greasing and oiling and repairing farm equipment so that it would run perfectly when the fieldwork began. When they weren't peering into tractor engines or sharpening cutting blades, they were talking about where and what cash crops—tobacco, corn, alfalfa, and hay—would be planted.

Indoors, March was "windowsill month." We carefully tucked seeds into dirt-filled cups and milk carton halves so they would sprout in the warming sun coming through the windowpanes. But potting the new seeds and nursing seedlings didn't always mean winter was over. In fact, we often had an "onion snow," that is, a heavy, wet, late-season snow that surprised us and the spring onions that already were in the ground.

The sight of this snow, which usually was quick to melt, made the adults grumble. But it never brought farm activities to a halt until the day my mother spotted some ghostly forms in the field belonging to our Amish neighbors. She looked out the window. She went back and looked again. She called my aunt and grandmother to look, too. She exclaimed, "I'm not one to waste camera film, but I've got to have a picture of this."

Her black and white photo, taken at the height of the storm, looked like someone had filled the air with a zillion goose-down feathers shaken from a pillow. But on second glance, we could see the shadowy forms of our neighbors guiding their four horses and plow through the field.

Farm families often engaged in friendly competition to see who could get their fields and gardens planted first and be the first to have new-season produce on the table. The race included our Amish friends, who often got a head start on us because their equipment was lighter and less likely to become mired in a muddy field than our tractor. Of course, my mother also had her own personal race. Her goal each year was to have sugar peas and new potatoes on the table in time for her mid-June anniversary dinner.

Late March and April were the times to work the ground that hadn't already been planted. Close to the house, we children helped our parents clean out the strawberry beds, removing old buds and dead leaves, and then covering the plants with straw to keep them from freezing at night.

Meanwhile, the men worked to prepare regular fields as well as those containing raised planting beds. The raised beds' soil was sterilized to a depth of about six inches, using steam created by a gasoline engine. Into this specially treated soil would go delicate tobacco seeds that would flourish in the weed-free beds. Not ones to waste good soil, we also planted some of our garden lettuce and spinach around the edges of the tobacco beds.

Kitchen gardens, closer to the house, were carefully measured off and planted with a surveyor's precision. Straight-as-an-arrow rows of all kinds of vegetables, as well as rectangular sweet corn plots, always were enclosed by flower borders. Even today, in travels around Lancaster County, spotting a garden completely surrounded by flowers is as much of a clue that you've come across an Amish farm as seeing a windmill and waterwheels generating power or observing horses and buggies on the property.

Although Mennonites like my family were no shirkers when it came to keeping farms neat, the Amish always have been known to take as much pride in the beauty of their fields and gardens as they do in the fruits of their harvest. As I understand it, they have a deep, basic belief in order in daily life, and that begins with a home that's well-kept, both indoors and out. Knowing that the entire Amish congregation was going to visit the house for services several times a year no doubt added to the importance of keeping everything neat. However, like the rest of us, the Amish still had last-minute details to take care of before church day, and sometimes worked until nearly midnight on the day before the congregation was to arrive. They wanted to make sure no one spotted a weed outdoors or a cobweb indoors.

We hurried to finish our own annual spring-cleaning ritual, too, because our outdoor tasks were growing daily. After the spring onion sets and peas were planted, the seeds for cutting lettuce, spinach, and white and red radishes went into the ground. Then came the first of many rounds of corn planting, so that we'd have the first ears by the Fourth of July. By the time the green tips of asparagus broke the ground's surface, and bright red strawberries were plump and ripe for picking, we were planting more and more. Next in the natural rhythm of plant, weed, and pick were the pole beans (which are bigger and flatter than Ford Hook limas), green beans, yellow wax beans, and Italian beans, to say nothing of cucumbers, peppers, and sweet potatoes. Whenever I didn't have my nose in a schoolbook, it seemed I was bent over and nose-down in the garden. I began to suspect the adults had ordered at least a dozen of every single item in the seed catalog.

As the days became warmer and the dark green watercress began emerging along the banks of the stream and pristine spring, my friends and I began having difficulty concentrating on our lessons at the North Star one-room school. Instead of taking our cold-morning quick route across the meadows, we took the long way to school so that we could spot patches of Johnny Jump Ups and watch the fuzzy white buds of pussy willow trees turn to leaves. On the way home, we were even more easily distracted, because we knew that more weeding and hoeing awaited us. Some of my friends kicked their metal lunch pails along the path. If one of us spotted an animal's footprints, we veered off on wild game hunts. Even checking the progress of the watercress became a diversion for me. Although the peppery cress was a favorite green for salads and added a gentle but intriguing "bite" to tomato juice, I loved it between two slices of buttered bread. Now that was a sandwich!

Scouting for the first delicate dandelion leaves to emerge in the meadows also was one of my more important responsibilities. But my parents had no intentions of running for the weed killer when I reported those first finds. Instead, they handed me a knife, and I busied myself cutting off the young plants where they emerged from the soil. When I arrived at home, my mother or aunt would clean the plants by stripping off the little bit of root still attached to the leaves and washing them before they were tossed in hot bacon dressing—an area specialty that may have inspired today's trendy wilted salads.

When dandelion plants began to flower, the leaves turned too bitter to eat. But there was much more to do with this wondrous weed. Although I'm not so sure I agree, some ladies claim batter-dipped dandelion flowers taste like oysters. I say "shucks" to the oyster idea, and advise tossing the blooms into crocks, along with sugar and raisins, to ferment and create dandelion wine.

Cutting lettuce and fresh spinach were the next greens to fill our salad bowls. But on other days, we nibbled our way through raw carrots, delicate baby radishes, and spring onions after dipping them in just a little salt. Crisp cucumber slices, crunchy pepper chunks, and celery sticks appeared on vegetable platters as the garden flourished.

There were daily chores to keep up with production. Because I was the smallest of the children on the farm, and therefore closest to the ground, I was on asparagus patrol. Any tip that dared to emerge overnight was mine in an

instant. "Aha, there's another one and another!" I'd say, and ruthlessly slash off spear after spear when they were just three to four inches long. Trouble is that the hotter the days were, the faster the asparagus grew. That's when I had to machete my way through the asparagus jungle at sunrise and again at sunset.

When I had leveled all the spears, I moved in to pull out baby beets and carrots that had dared to grow too close together. But the offenders weren't tossed onto the compost pile. Oh, no, that's not the way we Pennsylvanians are. Thanks to our sense of thrift, we treasured baby vegetables decades before famous chefs popularized the idea. If the tiny carrots or beets weren't steamed for dinner that night, they were pickled and canned.

There was, however, one task connected with baby vegetables that I abhorred—gathering gherkins as they formed from the blossoms on cucumber vines. Every leaf had to be lifted to spot these pint-sized pickles, and it was impossible to touch those leaves without winding up with a good case of "the itch." After a session in

they were pickled or provided the highlights in our special "company's coming" vegetable chow-chow—a pickled, sweet and sour relish composed of some of the best green beans, yellow beans, kidney beans, chopped celery, diced onion, and corn kernels that could be found in the garden.

More than once I got myself into hot water by snitching a few baby gherkins from the chow-chow intended for dinner guests. I would sneak into the dining room and carefully, ever so carefully, shift the other vegetables around to conceal the spaces where the baby gherkins had been. But I was found out by my mother who had enough detective skills to be the American version of Agatha Christie's Miss Marple.

We passed portions of the hottest summer days sitting on the back steps to do some of the kitchen work. We could catch the breeze, talk, and tease while "stringing" string beans and sugar peas and shelling regular peas or lima beans. We also could share views that spanned much more than a single kitchen window. As we worked, we could gaze at the cows in the pasture, the stand of trees by our swimming hole in the Pequea Creek, as well as get a chuckle from listening in on the conversations between Grandmother Herr and the Amish matriarch who lived next door. The two of them spent their days "supervising" the work and gliding back and forth in the two-seater lawn swing as they solved the problems of the world.

When tomatoes ripened, it seemed as if they were determined to swamp us in a red sea. After we'd savored the first ones sliced in sandwiches and diced for salads, we tackled the abundance in ways that would have amazed even the Italians who see them as part of the foundation for their much-heralded Mediterranean diet.

We crushed and served them over homemade noodles—our version of pasta and sauce. Other tomatoes were mixed with diced pepper, chopped onion, sugar and vinegar and thickened to create sweet-and-sour stewed tomatoes. Those tomatoes were good enough to stand

the vines, I felt like scratching everywhere, from the tips of my toes to my neck. The crowning touch was having to go from the cucumbers to the tomato plants. Those plants, which deposited a sticky, light green residue on my legs as I rubbed against them, made me scratch even more. Looking back, I believe my mother was onto something big. She discovered the ideal way to make a child beg to take a bath.

I had to temper my protests about searching the vines, however, because I loved those baby gherkins. They were irresistible when alone as an accompaniment to mild meats such as roast pork or chicken. But the stewed tomatoes became heavenly when they were poured into the centers of mounds of fluffy white mashed potatoes.

Still more of the tomato crop went into a smoky ketchup made by simmering the tomatoes for hours and hours and seasoning them with cloves, cinnamon, and sugar. In some ways, the end result was more like some of the barbecue sauces we use today.

Any tomatoes that stayed on the vine too long and became over-ripe were pressed and turned into regular tomato juice or seasoned with pureed watercress and freshly cracked peppercorns, creating a great version of vegetable juice for the winter months. The jars of juice helped fill shelves that already were lined with canned tomatoes in all possible forms, from crushed and whole to pureed and roughly chopped.

Another special treat was a meal of pan-fried tomatoes that were cut into slices about one-third of an inch thick, floured on both sides, and seasoned with salt and pepper before going into a frying pan coated with a blend of butter and vegetable oil. As the slices cooked, they were lightly sprinkled with brown sugar to help them caramelize and brown. The slices, which still delivered fresh tomato flavor in their centers, were so popular that the women had to spell each other at the stove if they, too, wanted to eat some.

Towards the end of tomato season, and when we were just about out of ideas, the occasional green tomato pie was baked. I viewed these creations, born of desperation during the Depression, as a culinary tragedy. The only positive thing to say for them is that the green tomatoes, when combined with cinnamon, cloves, nutmeg, and spices, stayed somewhat crunchy and made a better mock-apple pie than the famous one using Ritz crackers.

Corn was the only vegetable that got more

attention than tomatoes. We picked the ears in the cooler hours of early morning or after sundown, when the ears were at their sugary best, rather than starchy from baking in the hot sun.

When it was in season, corn-on-the-cob was on the table for each meal. We never tired of it because we had more ways to use corn than there were kernels on a cob. Custard-like corn pudding and creamed corn were excellent side dishes with poultry. Corn pies and corn and clam pies, savory creations with fillings bound by eggs and sandwiched between flaky crusts, were hearty enough to be a meal's main course.

More corn? No problem. We kept digging into our repertoire. Corn soup, with a base of chicken broth, became another meal with the addition of rivels (little bits of flour mixed with egg) that were like "instant" noodles.

Corn fritters were another pleasant way to whittle away at any overabundance of corn. Actually, they're best described as corn pancakes. Round and flat, they were nothing more than corn kernels mixed with eggs, flour, salt, and pepper, plus a little sugar to enhance the corn's sweetness. After the batter turned golden on the griddle, the corn cakes were served with thick golden molasses or with real maple syrup. Mother never used imitation pancake syrup because she said it was so runny it spread out and coated everything else on the plate.

Still more corn? We cut the corn from hundreds of cobs and froze it. But we also cut corn off dozens more cobs to make dried corn. This Pennsylvania specialty, when reconstituted in milk or cream and butter, tastes like no other corn you'll ever have. It goes with just about any country meat, from turkey and chicken to ham and sausage. It's also a congenial mixer, should it get too close to other foods on the plate like mashed potatoes or bread filling.

Making the dried corn was a task I particularly enjoyed. Although the corn was not intended as a snack, I loved to crunch the crisp kernels much like today's campers nibble trail mix. Although I would have liked to "hit" the dried corn the same way I sneaked the gherkins from the chow-chow, I behaved better as long as I could have an occasional handful.

Once we cut the kernels from the cob, they were spread out to dry on wire trays that fit on racks built around the sides of the coal stove. The stove had to be warm, but not hot. The oven was kept low as well. The drying corn filled the air with a wonderful aroma. No one ever resented the time it took to make it, even when it involved getting up in the middle of the night to turn it so the kernels would dry evenly on both sides. As the corn became drier and drier, the kernels became more crunchy and caramelized. I must confess that asking me to tend to the corn in the middle of the night was like leaving a burglar an open window of opportunity.

When the last of the dried corn was poured into two sacks of fine cotton and placed in large tin cans, our work canning and preserving the garden's vegetable bounty was just about over. But the tasks left a lasting impression on me. Although I no longer can vegetables out of necessity, I can't resist making some special pickles and relishes each year and putting up some fruits of my own. I understand the thrill and satisfaction my mother felt when the rainbow-assortment of vegetables in the jars were neatly arranged on the shelves to create a season's testimonial to the abundance of this land.

One evening when I was entertaining some of our Amish neighbors, I said to them, "I hope you will come down to the basement to see my canned vegetables and fruits and homemade wines because I'm very interested in keeping the tradition." After dinner, when the women followed me to the canning shelves, one said, "For you, this may be a tradition, but for us it is survival."

Previous Pages: The Amish of Lancaster County cultivate the soil by hand to plant flowers as well as vegetables. *Left:* Large, richly nutritious tomatoes are the result of a well-kept garden.

BASICS

BROWNED BUTTER

Enjoy the hearty, robust flavor of real butter by browning. You'll use half the butter and get twice the flavor. The nice part is that you may prepare $1/2$ to 1 pound at a time, refrigerate, and use a teaspoonful at a time. I use browned butter on all my vegetables, especially over mashed potatoes, pastas, eggs, and mild fish. Always use a deep saucepan for browning because the butter foams. Never leave the area after you start the process,

because the butter can easily burn. Start on medium heat and stir constantly. It will foam and begin to turn golden. As it quiets down, stir and watch carefully to keep it from burning. The butter should look light brown and have a caramel fragrance. Remove from heat before it burns, as it will lose its flavor and become bitter. It will be a rich nutty brown. After you experience this delight, you'll rarely use melted butter for topping again.

HOLLANDAISE SAUCE

2 large egg yolks (or 3 regular)
1 Tablespoon white wine
$1/2$ cup clarified butter
2 drops Tabasco sauce or hot sauce
$1/4$ teaspoon salt
$1/4$ teaspoon white or black pepper
2 Tablespoons fresh lemon juice
$1/2$ teaspoon zest of lemon rind

In top of double boiler or in mixing bowl,

combine egg yolks and wine, beating thoroughly. Place over boiling water, being careful not to cook the yolks, whisking until the egg mixture is warm. To clarify the butter, melt it and pour off the clear liquid. Slowly whisk in the butter until light and fluffy. Add the hot sauce, salt, pepper, lemon juice, and zest of lemon. Keep warm, not hot, or it will break (curdle). If it breaks, add another egg yolk and beat vigorously.

LEMON SAUCE

This is a great sauce for seafood or vegetables.

1 cup light cream
3 Tablespoons butter
1 teaspoon chopped mint leaves (if using dried, $1/2$ teaspoon)
$1/2$ teaspoon salt
2 egg yolks, lightly beaten
2 Tablespoons lemon juice
$1/2$ teaspoon grated (zest) lemon rind

In a 1-quart saucepan combine cream, butter, mint, and salt. Heat over low to medium heat until the butter is melted and mixture is hot. In a small bowl, beat the egg yolks. Spoon about $1/2$ cup of the heated mixture into the beaten egg yolks. Add to the remaining cream mixture in saucepan. Cook over low heat, stirring constantly with wooden spoon, for approx. 2 minutes or until thickened. Do not overcook, as sauce will curdle. Remove from heat, add lemon juice and rind. Served warm, it is delicious on seafood or vegetables.

BASICS

BAKED POTATOES – WHITE OR SWEET
ONE PER PERSON

Choose potatoes that are fresh, not wrinkled, and about the same size.

Scrub potatoes and prick with fork at least two times to prevent skin from exploding. I like a crisp crusty skin, so I may eat the center and then butter and season the skin—I suppose that is why "potato skins" are so popular. If you prefer a soft skin, rub with vegetable oil or butter, or an oil-based salad dressing will work if you like the flavors of herbs and spices.

Place potatoes in shallow baking pan, and put them in a preheated 400° F. oven, approx. 1 hour (if sweet potatoes, less time is needed) or until they seem soft when squeezed gently. Each variety of potato has a different consistency, so use your own judgment. The potato should be soft and tender inside. Slash through center, pressing both ends together to show the beauty and depth, giving room for any filling provided.

Serve with butter, salt, pepper, and any or all of your favorites—cheese, parsley, chives, sautéed mushrooms, chopped green onions, sour cream, minced ham, crumbled bacon, chopped bologna, or shaved and minced dried beef.

TOMATO SAUCE
SERVES 4 TO 6

4 cups fresh tomatoes or 3 cups canned, diced tomatoes—do not discard the liquid
$^1/_4$ cup butter
$^1/_3$ cup flour
1 teaspoon salt
$^1/_2$ teaspoon freshly ground black pepper
2 Tablespoons brown sugar, honey, or maple syrup
$^1/_2$ cup onion, finely chopped

In large saucepan, melt butter, add flour, salt, pepper, sugar and onion on medium heat, stirring until smooth. Add liquid from tomatoes. Bring to a boil and simmer for no more than a minute. Check for seasoning, adding more salt or sugar if desired. Add tomatoes and simmer until thoroughly heated.

POTATO FILLING
SERVES 6

This hearty side dish often accompanies roast chicken or turkey or an elegant baked ham.

$^1/_4$ cup butter or shortening
$^3/_4$ cup chopped celery and leaves
$^1/_2$ cup chopped onion
2 Tablespoons minced parsley or 1
   Tablespoon dried parsley
$^1/_2$ cup boiling water
Pinch of saffron
$^1/_2$ teaspoon salt
$^1/_2$ teaspoon freshly ground pepper
2 cups mashed potatoes
2 eggs, beaten until fluffy
2 cups bread cubes (croutons may be used)
1 cup milk, (but use $^1/_4$ cup more of milk if
   using croutons)
Butter for coating casserole and topping

In a deep skillet, sauté the celery, onion, and parsley in butter until tender. Add the water, saffron, salt, and pepper. Heat to nearly boiling. Then, lightly mix with the mashed potatoes, eggs, and bread cubes. Fold in the milk to blend everything. Remove from heat and pour into buttered casserole or soufflé dish and bake in preheated 350° F. oven for 40 minutes. Top with butter if desired, but serve promptly because it will drop in the center if cooled.

GOLDEN HARVEST SOUP
YIELDS: 8 CUPS

1/4 pound bacon or 4 slices
1 medium onion, chopped
2 stems celery, with leaves, chopped
1 small clove garlic, minced
1/2 teaspoon curry powder
1/4 teaspoon nutmeg
1/4 teaspoon white pepper
1/2 teaspoon salt
8 cups water
2 pounds butternut squash or neck
    pumpkin, peeled, seeded, and cut into
    2-inch chunks
3 large carrots, scrubbed and sliced
    (peeled if you prefer)
1 medium white potato, peeled and sliced
1 medium rutabaga, peeled and sliced
    (if unavailable, use white potato)
1/2 teaspoon salt
1/4 teaspoon fresh dill
1/4 teaspoon fresh thyme
1/4 teaspoon fresh basil (chop all three
    herbs finely—if using dried herbs, a pinch
    of each will do.)
1/3 cup rum (or 2 Tablespoons rum flavoring)
2 Tablespoons fresh lemon juice—zest the
    rind for garnish
1 Tablespoon sugar
Spiced whipped cream and lemon zest for
    topping, or sprigs of the fresh herbs

Fry the bacon until crisp in a heavy stockpot. Remove the bacon, place on paper towels to drain, and crumble. Set bacon aside. Add the onion, celery, garlic, curry, nutmeg, white pepper, and salt to the bacon fat and sauté over medium heat for 5 minutes. Add the water, squash, carrots, potato, rutabaga, and herbs.

Cover with lid and cook over medium heat for 45 minutes. Cool slightly and pour by batches into a food mill, food processor, or blender and coarsely process. Pour back into stockpot and stir in the rum, lemon juice, and sugar. Check for seasonings, adding salt and pepper if needed. Simmer slowly over low heat until bubbles appear on top, approx. 10 minutes. Do not bring to a full boil.

Serve hot with a dollop of Spiced Whipped Cream, or Spiced Sour Cream.

SPICED SOUR CREAM

8 ounces sour cream
2 Tablespoons light brown sugar or honey
Dash of nutmeg
Dash of cinnamon
Pinch of salt

Mix all the ingredients in a bowl until well blended. Cover with plastic wrap and refrigerate for a few hours.

Spiced Whipped Cream

Place 1 teaspoon curry powder and ¹/₂ teaspoon nutmeg in a small skillet or saucepan and heat over <u>low</u> heat until slightly dark and it smells great, approx. 2 minutes. Cool and fold into whipped cream.

DANDELION OR SPINACH SALAD WITH HOT BACON DRESSING
SERVES 4 TO 6

6 cups loosely packed young dandelion or spinach greens, roots trimmed, washed and cleaned

1/2 pound bacon—save 4 Tablespoons of the fat with brownings for dressing

4 hard-cooked eggs, peeled

Dressing:

2 Tablespoons cornstarch

1-1/2 teaspoons salt

3 Tablespoons granulated sugar

2 eggs

1/3 cup cider vinegar

2 cups milk

Tear the washed greens as you would for any garden salad and place in a bowl. Cook the bacon in the microwave or oven at 375° F. (approx. 5 minutes) until crisp. By laying the slices flat and covering with wax paper, the strips will remain flat. Dab the bacon with paper towel to remove excess fat. Cool and break into bite-size pieces or bits.

Dressing: Combine the cornstarch, salt, and sugar in a 1-quart saucepan. Slowly add the two eggs, stir or lightly beat, and gradually add the vinegar. Blend and stir in the milk and 4 tablespoons reserved bacon fat. Stir with a whip, wooden spoon, or spatula until it comes to a boil. Cool slightly, so as not to burn the tongue when eating. Pour some of the dressing over the salad. Serve the remainder in a side dish to pour over the salad. Top with the sliced hard-boiled eggs and the remaining bacon.

PUFFED POTATOES

This is one of the best ways to enjoy a healthy snack. They're quick, easy, and delicious. Baking potatoes are best suited for this use, but you can use almost any large potato. Scrub them well, cut inch–thick slices, and pop in a hot oven or toaster oven at 400° F. to 450° F. until they puff. There's no need to peel them, or use a baking pan. If they are placed on a clean rack they will be brown on both sides. When they are golden brown, they're ready to eat. I like to slit the top and slide a bit of butter inside. Add a bit of salt and pepper and enjoy while they are nice and hot.

To serve them as the starch for a meal, cut the slices thicker to retain the heat.

FRIED POTATOES—RAW (HOME) FRIES
SERVES 4 TO 6

2 pounds white potatoes or half white, half sweet
6 slices bacon or 1/4 cup shortening
1/2 teaspoon salt (optional)
1/2 teaspoon coarsely ground black pepper
1 medium-size onion, thinly sliced or chopped (optional)
1 Tablespoon chopped fresh chives
Approx. 1/3 cup water, divided
Fresh chopped chives or fresh onion rings for garnish

The secret to home fries that are crispy outside and soft inside is the use of water and a lid while frying. It makes all the difference.

Scrub potatoes, peel if desired, and slice to desired thickness. A food processor works great, as does a mandoline. Fry the bacon until crisp. Remove bacon and dry on paper towels. If using shortening, melt on medium heat. Add sliced potatoes, salt, pepper, onion, and chives. When the potatoes are golden, turn and sprinkle with a tablespoon of water. Cover and repeat, turning occasionally to prevent burning. Each time you turn the potatoes, sprinkle with water before covering with the lid. Fry until they are golden brown on each side, approx. 25 minutes.

MASHED POTATOES
SERVES 4 TO 6

3 pounds white potatoes, washed, peeled, and quartered
1-$\frac{1}{2}$ teaspoons salt
1 quart of water or enough to cover potatoes
4 to 6 Tablespoons butter
$\frac{1}{3}$ cup evaporated milk
$\frac{2}{3}$ cup milk, heated
$\frac{1}{4}$ teaspoon freshly ground pepper
Browned butter for topping

Place potatoes in large saucepan, add the salt and water. Bring to a boil, cover, and cook until soft, approx. 30 minutes. Remove potatoes with slotted spoon and put in a large mixing bowl. With beater on low, add the butter and slowly add the evaporated milk, heated milk and pepper. Whip until very fluffy. Check for seasoning, adding more salt and pepper if desired. Serve in heated dish. Top with browned butter (recipe on page 21).

Warning: New and red skin potatoes will not whip as well as the baking varieties. Kennebec, Idaho, and Irish Cobbler are my favorites. Make plenty of mashed potatoes because any leftovers are great for another meal, made into potato filling, or potato pancakes, or used as a thickening for cream soups.

SWEET POTATO CROQUETTES
SERVES 4

1 pound sweet potatoes
1 teaspoon salt
2 cups water
2 eggs, lightly beaten
$\frac{1}{4}$ cup honey
$\frac{1}{4}$ cup butter or margarine
1 egg, beaten, with 1 Tablespoon milk and $\frac{1}{4}$ cup water
Dried bread crumbs, approx. 1 cup
Butter or shortening for frying

Boil the potatoes in salted water until tender, approx. 20 minutes. Remove from water and peel. Mash or puree and add beaten egg, honey, and shortening, blending well. Chill until firm enough to form. Form into balls, logs, or cones. Dip in beaten egg and milk mixture, then roll in bread crumbs. If you prefer a thicker coating, chill and repeat again—this is best if you're freezing them. Brown in heavy skillet on medium heat, adding shortening if needed. Remove, drain on paper towels and arrange on platter. If you are freezing the croquettes, thaw and bake at 375° F. for approx. 12 minutes or until a fork, inserted into the middle, is hot.

When freezing, it is very easy to package the amount you want by placing croquettes on a baking sheet. When frozen, remove and put in freezer bags. Mark and date each bag.

Serve with gravy, wine, sherry sauce, or a curried fruit compote.

ASPARAGUS AND NEW POTATOES

1 pound fresh asparagus, bottoms trimmed
4 slices bacon (optional)
1 clove garlic, crushed or thinly sliced
2 cups red skin potatoes, balled
   with melon baller or cubed
$^1/_2$ teaspoon salt
$^1/_4$ teaspoon white pepper

Hold each stem of asparagus in your hand, snapping the bottom where it breaks. If it is "right from the garden" there will be very little waste. The portion of stem below the "breaking point" is tough and fibrous. Discard these ends or save them to toss into a stock-pot of vegetables.

In heavy skillet or wok, simmer bacon until golden and crisp. Remove and drain on paper towels. Save half the fat to stir-fry. If not using bacon, add olive oil, approx. 2 Tablespoons. Add garlic and potatoes, cover with lid, reduce heat to medium, and stir occasionally until potatoes are golden brown and medium soft, approx. 3 minutes. Leave trimmed asparagus stems whole or cut into diagonal slices about 1 to 1-$^1/_2$" long. Add asparagus, salt and pepper.

Cover for one minute, check for seasoning, and crumble bacon over top. If it is too crunchy, continue simmering for another minute or two. If you prefer, toast tips or croutons are great as a garnish, so enjoy!

*A*s a young girl, my garden chore was to cut the asparagus each day. To gain more tips and assure the quality and taste, the stems had to be cut in the early morning and late in the afternoon. For reasons only children would understand, I vowed I would never like or eat asparagus. Once I married Abe and it was the first vegetable he wanted to plant in our new garden (stating that it was his favorite), I knew it would be wise to learn to appreci- ate the taste. I suppose I didn't like it because we overcooked it; therefore, I had to find a way to savor the "special" veg- etable. This is my version.

DRIED CORN IN CREAM
SERVES 6

*M*y family dried corn each summer. I could hardly wait until corn was ready, as it is one of my favorites. It has a unique flavor; one would think it has a caramel flavoring added. When corn is dried properly, the sweetness is retained without adding any sugar. It is one of the definite Pennsylvania Dutch specialties. Now you can purchase "John Cope's Dried Sweet Corn" through the Internet (http://www.copefoods.com). It is so good, and is much easier than drying your own.

1 cup dried corn
2 cups milk
1-1/2 teaspoons salt
1 teaspoon sugar (optional)
2 Tablespoons butter
1 cup cream, half and half, or milk

In a 1-1/2 quart container, soak the dried corn in the two cups of milk overnight, covered, in the refrigerator. Thirty minutes before serving, place the corn mixture in a 2-quart saucepan and add the rest of the ingredients. Bring to a near boil, reduce heat to low, and simmer for 30 minutes, stirring occasionally to prevent sticking. Enjoy!

BAKED CORN PUDDING
SERVES 4 TO 6

2-1/2 cups fresh or frozen corn
   (whole kernels or creamed)
1 Tablespoon sugar or honey (optional)
1 teaspoon salt
1/4 teaspoon pepper
1 Tablespoon parsley, finely chopped
2 Tablespoons flour
1/4 cup melted butter
3 eggs, lightly beaten
1/4 cup cream or evaporated milk
1 cup milk

If corn is frozen, let it thaw. Combine all the ingredients and pour into an oiled or buttered 1-1/2- to 2-quart baking dish. Bake in a pre-heated 350° F. oven for 35 to 40 minutes, or until golden brown on top.

This freezes well if it is not over–baked. Cool properly before sealing and freezing.

ACORN SQUASH WITH TURKEY STUFFING
SERVES 4

2 4″ fall squash
4 Tablespoons melted butter
1/2 teaspoon salt and pepper to taste
Water for baking

Wash and cut each squash in half—in the middle. Scoop out seeds and trim the bottoms of each half to ensure them standing straight while baking. Brush each inside with butter. Sprinkle lightly with salt and pepper. Place in baking dish. Add water to baking dish until halfway up the squash. Bake at 350° F. for approx. 45 min. or until tender when tested with a fork. Remove from oven. Drain and fill with turkey stuffing.

Turkey Loaf or Stuffing:
1 tablespoon butter
1/3 cup chopped celery
1/3 cup chopped onion
3 strips bacon

Sauté celery, onion, and bacon with butter until lightly browned. Remove bacon and cut in small pieces. In mixing bowl crumble the bacon.

1 lb. fresh ground turkey
2 eggs, lightly beaten
1/3 cup milk
1-1/2 cups fresh bread crumbs
1/2 cup apple butter
1/2 teaspoon black pepper
1 teaspoon salt
1 Tablespoon chopped pimento
1/2 teaspoon chopped chervil
   (parsley may be substituted)
1/2 teaspoon lemon pepper
1 teaspoon chopped chives
2 Tablespoons vegetable oil or butter
1/3 cup fruit jelly or jam for topping
Parsley for garnish

Blend turkey with celery and bacon mixture and the rest of the ingredients except the oil or butter and jam topping. Toss until well-mixed. Add oil or butter to skillet and stir meat mixture until lightly browned.

Fill the squash, rounding generously. If there is extra stuffing, form into loaf and bake in small baking dish. Bake at 350° F. for approx.15 minutes. Add jam and continue baking until loaf and squash are browned and crusty, approx. 20 minutes. Serve while very hot. Garnish with parsley if desired.

GLAZE FOR VEGETABLES

There is nothing better than fresh vegetables, steamed, or par cooked with a glaze or sauce to complement a meal. I love a tinge of spices, fruit juice or zest, or dried fruits with vegetables. By combining your favorites, artichokes, beans, beets, cabbage, carrots, cauliflower, broccoli, Brussels sprouts, eggplant, onions, peas, peppers, potatoes, kohlrabi, leeks, red cabbage, rutabaga, parsnips, salsify, spinach, turnips, squash, sweet potatoes, tomatoes, yams and zucchini become your special dishes.

^{1}/$_3$ **cup butter**
^{1}/$_2$ **cup sugar, white or brown**
^{1}/$_2$ **cup honey or maple syrup**
^{1}/$_4$ **teaspoon nutmeg, cinnamon & spice (optional)**
Zest of lemon, orange, lime or grapefruit
^{1}/$_3$ **cup white wine, apple or grape juice**
Salt and pepper to taste

Melt butter in a heavy skillet. Add sugar, honey, spices, and zest of citrus. Stir on medium heat, until sugar is dissolved, turning a light golden color. Add wine or juice and heat thoroughly. Add salt and pepper to taste. Pour over vegetables and serve piping hot in nice serving dish.

Hint: This glaze may be made ahead and refrigerated for a week. If freezing, do not add the wine until glaze is thawed. When ready to serve, add wine to the glaze. Stir until thoroughly heated. Pour over vegetables and serve immediately.

BAKED CABBAGE
SERVES 4

1 medium-size cabbage
$^1/_2$ cup water
2 Tablespoons flour
$^1/_2$ teaspoon salt
$^1/_2$ teaspoon ground pepper
1 Tablespoon sugar
3 Tablespoons butter
1 cup milk, heated
$^1/_2$ cup grated cheese—cheddar, American
  and Swiss

Core the cabbage and cut in wedges. In saucepan, add water and cabbage. Cover and steam until slightly tender, approx. 4 minutes. Drain well and place in buttered baking dish. Combine flour, salt, pepper, and sugar. Sprinkle over the cabbage. Melt butter in saucepan and add the milk. Pour over cabbage and top with cheese. Bake in a pre-heated 350° F. oven for 35 minutes or until golden brown and bubbling around sides.

RHUBARB CRUMBLE
SERVES 6

3 cups diced rhubarb (never use the leaves)
$^3/_4$ cup granulated sugar
$^1/_4$ cup water
1 Tablespoon lemon juice
1 cup brown sugar
Pinch of salt
1-$^1/_2$ cups flour
$^1/_2$ cup butter or margarine
Ice cream or whipped cream for topping
  (optional)

Mix the rhubarb, granulated sugar, water, and lemon juice and place in buttered 9-inch baking dish. Mix the brown sugar, salt, flour, and butter with your fingers or pastry blender until crumbly. Sprinkle evenly over the rhubarb and bake in preheated 350° F. oven for 40 minutes. Serve warm or cold, with or without whipped cream or ice cream.

HEN HOUSE

✦✦✦✦✦✦✦✦✦✦✦✦✦✦✦✦

*O*ur chickens may not have laid golden eggs, but they certainly helped me fill my piggy bank. When I was 12 and needed pocket money for important things like the latest Nancy Drew mysteries and root beer floats at the soda fountain in Strasburg, I asked my Dad if I could start my own little business. Not one to discourage a fledgling entrepreneur, Dad told me I could go ahead with my plans to clean out an old hen house and start using it again to raise chickens. Meanwhile, my eight-year-old cousin Dick got into the fowl business, too, by raising Muscovy and Peking ducks.

My personal flock would contain rusty-red-colored Rhode Island Reds and gray and white Bard Rocks—big-breasted, meaty birds that each laid a nice-sized brown egg every day. But to get started, I first needed to fool my mother's favorite "clucks" (motherly hens) into hatching chicks for me. Carefully, I slipped some hand-blown glass eggs into their nests to keep them "broody" while they produced eggs of their own.

Each day the hens laid additional fresh eggs, I'd make room for them by removing an equal number of glass eggs from their nests.

Because I had six hens "working" for me, I was able to fill the hen house in no time. There were a dozen straw-filled boxes or "nests" in

each of two rows that the hens obligingly filled with eggs. But my challenge was gathering those eggs before my own chickens became too motherly and produced more chicks than I could use.

So what could be so difficult about collecting eggs? My chickens definitely weren't as nasty as the geese our Amish neighbors had. Those birds truly are the "attack dogs" of the fowl family. Cross a hissing, squawking goose by failing to give it the handful of cracked corn it wants, and you'll wind up dropping all of it. Everything else is forgotten when a goose chomps down on your leg, biting with the fine little teeth in its beak and twisting and turning its head to do more damage. After an experience like that, I sympathized with Mark Twain, who immortalized one such fowl for biting off his back pocket.

My chickens weren't as mean as our other neighbors' free-ranging guinea and bandy hens, either. Those tough little birds, apparently nursing king-sized Napoleon complexes, believed they were every bit as big and tough as the geese. Walk an inch off the side of the road and onto "their" property and they'd do their best to get a nip at you.

The key to collecting my daily "take" of eggs was getting into the hen house when the roosters were off-guard. When these guys

Left: When I was young, chickens normally ranged freely in and around the chicken house.

weren't shrilly heralding the dawning of each new day, they busied themselves strutting, preening, and keeping an eye on their "girls." Just being in the hen house, let alone reaching for an egg, wasn't a good idea when they were around. They usually flapped their wings, which really didn't scare me. It was upsetting, however, when they were riled enough to start pecking my skirt or flying up to give my pony-tail a good, hard pull.

I could wait only so long for the roosters to wander off on their own, because egg-gathering was only one of my daily chores. Occasionally, I had to scatter a handful of cracked corn and wheat to distract them from their responsibilities. Then I'd steal into the hen house to outfox the hens, too. It took just a few seconds to put a hen at ease by rubbing her head, the same way I'd pet a kitten. She'd either hop right off the nest to show me her latest egg or simply overlook the fact that while one hand was stroking her head, the other was fishing around underneath her in search of her egg.

When I had time to spare, I repaid the hens by practicing a relaxation technique on them. All I had to do was gently stroke a chicken between the eyes and before long, she'd tuck her head beneath her wing to catch a little shut-eye. It even works outdoors, in case you ever manage to catch a chicken that needs soothing!

My hens also served as foster mothers, although this responsibility sometimes ruffled their feathers. Each spring when the meadow surrounding my hen house needed mowing, Dick and I would stand by while my father or uncle began cutting the weeds and meadow grass. We'd run when they signaled they had come across a nest of wild duck eggs. We knew the mother ducks would never return so we rescued the greenish-blue eggs in a basket and kept them warm with a towel until we could sneak them into the hens' nests for hatching.

The hens never minded that the eggs were different. They even overlooked the differences in their newly-hatched little broods. But there was trouble when the chicks and ducklings were old enough to go on their first meadow excursions for bugs and worms. One minute, the mother hens were marching at the head of a column of chicks and ducklings in neat, nursery school rows. Chaos would fly through the ranks, however, when the ducklings leaped into the meandering stream beside the path. As they plopped into the water and began paddling away, the mother hens would run along the bank, hysterically clucking and scolding these little runaways. In their minds, no doubt, they weren't debating the "which came first, the chicken, the duck, or the egg" question, but were pondering how they could have produced such wayward and misguided offspring.

Although I sold my chickens and eggs, my mother and aunt (with ample advice from my grandmother) always used the main hen house's production for all kinds of good foods.

Eggs showed their fun-side when they weren't being scrambled or fried sunny-side-up. In summer, they were served as "deviled" eggs (hard-boiled egg halves filled with a mixture of mashed egg yolk, mustard, vinegar, mayonnaise, and other seasonings) or turned a wild shade of magenta when used for pickled beets and eggs. Either type of eggs was a welcome addition to a picnic table laden with baked chicken, corn-on-the-cob, potato salad, baked beans, sliced tomatoes, and scallions. When our family cooks wanted to prepare food on the wild side, they sometimes crossed the two ideas by making the deviled eggs' filling and stuffing it into pickled egg halves!

Saffron could be used to color and flavor anything that had wings, according to my mother. Although its price has always matched its golden color, a very small amount goes a long way. A single strand, actually the dried stamen plucked from a purple crocus, is enough to color a dish. We'd drop a strand into chicken soup or into the broth used for bread stuffing. Like many other Lancaster County cooks, we wouldn't think of serving chicken corn soup

without brightening the pot with the addition of saffron. It still is added to our restaurant's signature dish, Chicken Stoltzfus, and remains a key ingredient in hearty chicken pot pie.

In Pennsylvania Dutch country, pot pie doesn't mean chicken baked into a flaky pie crust. It's a wintertime poultry stew that contains homemade square egg noodles, along with boneless chicken chunks, potatoes, rich broth, and parsley, as well as saffron.

It takes time and several steps to make the pot pie because chickens first have to be cooked to create a rich broth. Next, the meat needs to be separated from the bones and the broth is strained. Finally, the noodles need to be dropped into the boiling broth, one-by-one, so that they don't stick together. Once all the noo-

dles are cooked, the chicken chunks are added to the broth and the dish is ready to serve.

My aunt, known for the lightness of her pot pie noodles, suddenly developed a problem with this relatively fail-safe dish. When she put me in charge of cooking the noodles, more and more of them stuck together. They weren't delicate and thin. They were thick and doughy, which was the way I liked them.

When she finally realized that I was the saboteur, she said, "Why didn't you just tell me?" From that day onwards, my portion always included a stack of doughy noodles, along with chicken in saffron-tinted broth. It also was the day I decided our chicken pot pie is the closest thing you'll ever find to a Pennsylvania Dutch pot of gold.

Above: Chicken pot pie and strawberry shortcake were frequent dishes at my childhood home.

ROAST CHICKEN WITH BREAD STUFFING
SERVES 6

This is so basic, popular, and easy that you'll make it often, each time using your own flair. The carcass and back pieces make excellent soup stock.

One 5 to 6 pound roasting chicken
1 teaspoon salt or herbal salt substitute
$^{1}/_{2}$ teaspoon pepper

Stuffing:
4 cups bread cubes
2 eggs, lightly beaten
$^{1}/_{3}$ cup milk
Dash of salt and pepper
$^{1}/_{2}$ cup celery, coarsely chopped
Tiny pinch of saffron (about 3 to 4 strands)

Remove the pouch of giblets and rinse chicken inside and outside. Pat dry. Sprinkle lightly with salt and pepper—inside and out. If you like giblet gravy, rinse and place the giblets in a saucepan, add 1 cup water and a dash of salt and pepper. Simmer on low heat until tender. Some folks do not like the liver, so I recommend keeping it separate. When the giblets are tender, remove and cut into small pieces to add to the gravy.

Mix all the stuffing ingredients together in a large bowl. Stuff the chicken gently so the stuffing will not be too heavy. Truss with cord or large toothpicks. If you have any extra stuffing, bake it in a greased baking dish until golden, to serve on the side.

Place the chicken in roasting pan, breast down. This prevents the white meat from becoming dry. Add $^{1}/_{2}$-cup water, tent with foil, and bake in preheated 375° F. oven for 3 hours. Uncover, turn breast side up to brown, and continue baking for 15 to 30 minutes. Remove and place on platter to serve. Remove the stuffing and arrange around the bird.

Gravy:
2 cups water
Giblet broth
4 Tablespoons corn starch
$^{1}/_{2}$ cup cold water
Chopped giblets
Salt and pepper

To make gravy, skim the fat from the broth in roaster. Deglaze with the water and the giblet broth and add the cornstarch dissolved in water, stirring until all the brownings are dissolved and the gravy thickens. Add the giblets. Check for seasonings and add salt and pepper if desired. Serve in gravy boat.

BASICS

MOIST HERB STUFFING

4 cups bread cubes
$^1/_2$ cup celery, coarsely chopped
1 teaspoon chervil, chopped fresh,
   or $^3/_4$ teaspoon if dried
1 teaspoon tarragon, chopped fresh,
   or $^1/_2$ teaspoon if dried
1 teaspoon parsley, chopped fresh,
   or $^1/_2$ teaspoon if dried
1 Tablespoon chives, chopped fresh,
   or $^1/_2$ teaspoon if dried
$^1/_4$ cup onion, chopped
1 cup chicken broth
$^1/_4$ teaspoon pepper
4 Tablespoons butter

Mix all the ingredients but the butter in a large bowl, tossing lightly. Spoon into generously buttered baking dish and dot with butter. Bake in preheated 350° F. oven for 30 to 40 minutes. The top should be golden brown.

This recipe is great for stuffing pork chops, poultry, or as an accompaniment to the main dish.

BASIC CHICKEN STOCK

3 pounds chicken pieces—backs, wings,
   necks, etc., including hearts and gizzards,
   but no livers (keep them for pate)
4 cups water
Pinch of saffron
1-$^1/_2$ teaspoons salt
1 teaspoon pepper
$^1/_2$ teaspoon thyme, chopped
Pinch of tarragon
$^1/_2$ cup celery, with leaves, chopped—use
   the root as well if available
$^1/_2$ cup onion, chopped
$^1/_4$ cup parsley, chopped

In a large stockpot, place all the ingredients and bring to a boil. Reduce heat to low and simmer for at least one hour. Strain through double cheesecloth. Cool and refrigerate. If you are freezing the stock, be sure to seal properly and label each container with date, etc.

CHICKEN STOLTZFUS
SERVES 6

1 large roasting chicken (approx. 5 pounds), cleaned, giblets removed
Water to cover, at least 1-1/2 quarts
2 teaspoons salt
1/2 teaspoon black pepper
Pinch of saffron, crushed

In heavy stockpot, add the chicken, water, salt, pepper, and saffron and bring to a boil. Partially cover, simmering on medium heat for 1 hour or until tender and legs separate easily from body. Remove chicken, debone, and remove skin. Strain the broth and skim off the fat. Reduce (or boil down) to about 4 cups of broth while chicken is cooling. Cut meat into bite-size pieces. Set aside.

Sauce:

3/4 cup butter or part margarine
3/4 cup flour
4 cups broth
1 cup light cream or 1/2 cup each of milk and evaporated milk

1/4 cup finely chopped fresh parsley or 1/8 cup dried parsley
Pre-baked pastry squares using pie crust recipe on page 117
Cubed chicken
Parsley for garnish

In deep pan or pot, melt the butter, stir in the flour. Cook over medium heat until it bubbles and is golden. Add the strained broth and cream, stirring constantly. Cook until sauce comes to a boil. Simmer until thickened and smooth. Reduce heat and add the chicken and parsley.

Serve on heated platter by placing pre-baked pastry squares on the bottom and sides of the platter. Pour the chicken mixture over the pastry, garnish and serve at once. The marvel of this dish is the combination of the chicken and flaky pastry. If left to stand, the pastry will gradually absorb the sauce.

CHICKEN POT PIE
SERVES 6 TO 8

1 4 to 6 pound roasting chicken
Tiny pinch of saffron (only about 3 to
  4 strands)
1 Tablespoon salt
1/2 teaspoon black pepper
About 2 quarts water
1/2 cup celery, coarsely chopped
1/4 cup parsley, chopped
2 medium potatoes, peeled and thinly sliced

Pot Pie Dough:
2-1/2 cups flour
2 eggs
1/3 cup water
1 Tablespoon butter
1/2 teaspoon salt

*W*e Pennsylvania Dutch have many unique dishes that are misinterpreted by the rest of the world. When we speak of "pot pie," we are referring to the large squares of noodle dough that are added to the boiling broth of the meat or vegetables. We always added a pinch of saffron to any chicken dish. Although saffron is the most expensive spice in the world, we feel it is worth it. It gives the poultry a rich golden color, an enhanced flavor when used with caution, and should be very delicate. The secret to a successful "slippery pot pie" is to make certain that pieces of the dough are not dropped on top of one another until the broth has boiled up over each layer. Pasta machines have made it much easier to make this wonderful dish. The dough squares may be prepared ahead. Dry them thoroughly and store in an airtight container in a dry place until ready to use.

Place the chicken in a 4-6 quart Dutch oven or a large heavy pot with a tight-fitting lid. Add the saffron, salt, and pepper, and enough water to just cover the bird. Bring to a boil, then reduce the heat and simmer about 1-1/4 hours until the chicken is tender. Remove the chicken from the broth. When cool enough to handle, remove skin, debone, and cut into large bite-sized chunks. Set aside while making pot pie dough.

Mound the flour on a pastry board or marble slab and make a well in the center. Break the eggs into this well. Add the water, butter, and salt. Gradually work the flour into the other ingredients until well blended. Gather into a ball and knead the dough until very tender, smooth, and elastic. Cover with a bowl or plastic wrap for several minutes. Divide into comfortable portions to roll.

Generously flour the board and top of the dough and roll the dough very thin—1/8 inch thick. The thinner the dough, the more delicate the dish. When using a pasta machine, use the same approach. Cut the dough into 2-inch squares. Do not stack the squares unless they are between wax paper.

recipe continued next page

CHICKEN POT PIE

Bring the chicken broth, celery, parsley, and potatoes to a boil over high heat. Drop the pot pie squares into the boiling broth in layers, being careful not to put a second layer in the pot until the boiling broth has covered the first one. As the pot is filled, push the squares down with a fork. Cook squares on low for about 10 to 12 minutes, stirring occasionally, until tender.

I like to heat most of the chicken separately and place it around a deep platter, only adding enough meat to the dough to make it look attractive. Add some of the small pieces of meat to the boiling dough and simmer for a few minutes. To serve use a deep platter, casserole dish, or baking dish. Place dough in middle, then add the heated chicken around the edge. Garnish with parsley or celery leaves.

TURKEY CROQUETTES OR CHICKEN TIMBALES
SERVES 4

These are so tender and delicate, and are excellent as an appetizer.

1-$^1/_2$ cups diced, cooked turkey or chicken
$^1/_4$ cup celery, finely diced
   (with leaves if desired)
$^1/_4$ teaspoon celery salt
$^1/_4$ teaspoon onion or garlic salt (optional)
1 teaspoon lemon juice
1 teaspoon parsley, finely chopped
$^1/_2$ cup thick white sauce (see note)
$^1/_2$ teaspoon salt
2 cups crumbs (half dried or toasted bread
   and half saltine crackers, crushed)
2 eggs, beaten
Fresh parsley for garnish
Sauce for dipping (optional)

In a large mixing bowl, combine the turkey or chicken, celery, celery salt, onion or garlic salt, lemon juice, parsley, white sauce, and salt. Form into cone–shaped croquettes or your favorite shape. Place the crumbs into a deep dish or pie pan. Roll croquettes in crumbs, then dip in beaten eggs, then roll in crumbs again. Chill for at least 30 minutes until firm. Deep-fry in oil preheated to 375° F. until golden brown. Keep warm in low oven until ready to serve. Serve with gravy or, if used as an appetizer, your favorite dipping sauce. Garnish with fresh parsley or sprigs of herbs.

Note: For white sauce, melt $^1/_2$ cup butter in saucepan. Stir in $^1/_4$ cup flour and $^1/_4$ cup milk. Keep stirring over low to medium heat until smooth and thick.

CORNMEAL FRIED CHICKEN WITH HERBS
SERVES 4 TO 6

4 boneless, skinless chicken breasts
¹/4 cup milk
1 egg, lightly beaten
¹/2 cup flour
¹/2 cup cornmeal
1 teaspoon salt
¹/2 teaspoon pepper
1 Tablespoon finely chopped fresh tarragon
1 Tablespoon finely chopped fresh chervil
   or parsley
2 Tablespoons butter
¹/4 cup vegetable oil
Fresh herbs for garnish

Cut chicken breasts in half. Mix milk and beaten egg in large bowl. Combine flour, cornmeal, salt, pepper, tarragon, and chervil or parsley in a large plastic or paper bag.

Dip chicken breast halves into milk and egg mixture. Then drop chicken pieces, one by one, into the bag containing flour and seasonings. Shake the pieces of chicken in the bag until well-coated. Place butter and oil in a heavy skillet or electric frying pan on medium heat. Place chicken in the pan and fry until golden on each side. Cover and continue to cook on medium-low heat for about 20 minutes, turning occasionally. Then remove cover and cook until the crust is crisp.

This recipe is good for any kind of poultry, especially Cornish hens, although cooking times will vary.

CHICKEN CORN SOUP
SERVES 6

One 4-pound roaster chicken,
  giblets removed
Water to cover, 6 to 8 cups
Pinch of saffron
2 teaspoons salt
$^1/_2$ teaspoon pepper

In a large pot, place the chicken and water, saffron, salt, and pepper. Cover, bring to a boil and simmer until tender, approx. 45 minutes. Remove chicken to cool. Strain and keep broth (you will need 2 cups of broth for soup). Remove skin, debone, and cut chicken in bite-sized pieces. If you want to have a good stock, cover bones with water, salt lightly, add a diced onion, and 1/2 teaspoon pepper, simmering for several hours on low heat. Measure 2 cups of chicken for use in soup. The remainder may be used in a vegetable or main dish. Refrigerate or freeze remainder for other recipes.

2 cups chicken broth
2 cups corn kernels (fresh or frozen)
1 cup celery with leaves, diced
1 Tablespoon chopped parsley
1 cup egg noodles, broken in pieces
Salt and pepper to taste
Garnish with parsley or sprig of
  fresh oregano
Sliced hard-cooked egg if desired

In large kettle, bring the chicken broth, corn, celery, parsley, and noodles to a boil, simmering for at least 5 minutes. Add the chicken and taste. Add salt, pepper or celery salt if needed. Garnish. Serve hot with hot buttered bread or crackers.

QUICHE
SERVES 6

1 9" pastry crust

1-1/2 cups shredded cheddar or Swiss
cheese (chilled cheese is easier to shred)

8 slices crisp bacon, crumbled

1/4 cup onions, chopped

1 cup mushrooms (portobellos) cleaned
w/paper towel or soft cloth and sliced

2 Tablespoons parsley, chopped

1 cup chicken, cooked and diced
(optional)

1 Tablespoon flour

1/2 teaspoon salt

4 eggs

1-1/2 cups light cream

Prebake the pastry crust for 5 minutes in a
preheated 350° F. oven; this prevents it from
becoming soggy. Sprinkle the cheese evenly
over the pastry shell. Grill or fry the bacon
until crisp. Remove the bacon and drain on
paper towels. Crumble the bacon and add to
cheese. Use a small amount of bacon fat to
sauté the onions, mushrooms, and parsley
until golden brown. Add the chicken, if
desired. Pour mixture over the cheese and
bacon. Mix flour and salt and sprinkle over
vegetables. Beat the eggs lightly in a bowl.
Add the cream. Pour over the cheese mixture.
Bake in 375° F. oven for 45 minutes, or until
firm and golden brown. Serve warm.

DEVILED EGGS
SERVES 8

6 to 8 large hard-cooked eggs, peeled
1 Tablespoon Dijon mustard
2 Tablespoons mayonnaise
$1/2$ teaspoon salt
$1/4$ teaspoon pepper
Paprika
Parsley or sliced olives for garnish

Cut eggs in half lengthwise and remove yolks, being careful not to break the whites.

In a small bowl, combine yolks, mustard, mayonnaise, salt and pepper. Beat until smooth and creamy. Check for seasoning, adding more salt or pepper if desired. Fill the egg whites with the yolk mixture by using a cake decorator tube or teaspoon. Sprinkle a bit of paprika on each just before serving. Garnish with parsley (chopped) or sliced olives.

PICKLED RED BEET EGGS

6 hard cooked eggs, peeled
1 pint of pickled herb beets or pickled beets (purchased from grocery)

Place eggs in a glass container with lid. Pour beet liquid over the eggs. Place some beets on top to keep the eggs covered. Cover and refrigerate for at least 12 hours—the longer they are in the beet liquid, the brighter red the eggs will be. These will keep in the refrigerator for at least a week.

When ready to serve, remove the eggs, drain and slice in halves lengthwise, using a clean, sharp knife. Make one cut, as dragging the knife through the egg will cause the beet juice to creep into the yolk. Serve cut side up with beets around the side. Garnish and be sure to have salt, pepper, and mustard available nearby.

GREAT MERINGUE
YIELDS: ENOUGH TO COVER A 9-INCH PIE

$2/3$ cup egg whites (approx. 6 large egg whites)
$1/2$ cup granulated sugar
$1/3$ teaspoon cream of tartar
$1/4$ teaspoon salt

Combine all the ingredients in a large mixing bowl. Place over a pan of hot water and stir briskly until mixture feels slightly warm to the back of your hand or finger, about 15 seconds.* Remove the bowl from the water and beat with a mixer (making sure the beaters are clean and free of fat) on high speed until the meringue holds firm peaks, about 1 to 2 minutes. Do not over–beat or the meringue will be dry and hard to spread on top puddings, pies or fruit tarts. Broil briefly or bake at 370° until peaks are golden.

*This tip was shared by my friend Marion Cunningham, well-known cookbook author and distinguished cooking teacher.

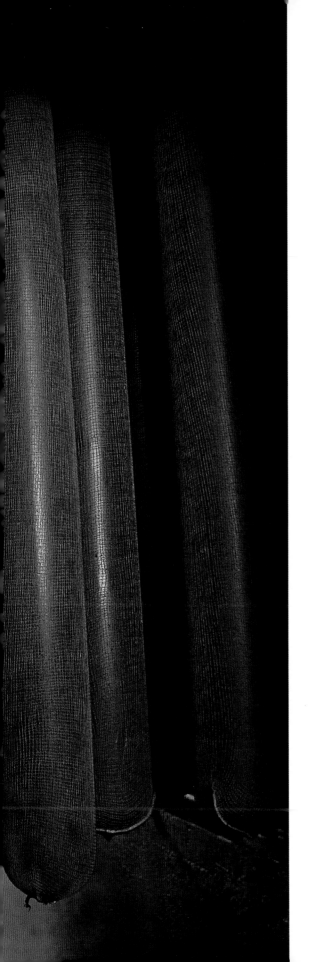

BUTCHER SHOP

■◆■◆■◆■◆■◆■◆■◆■◆■◆■

*G*ray curls of smoke always make me think of the autumns of my childhood, but not because I was filled with a burning desire to go back to school.

Smoke rising from mounds of golden, copper, red, brown, and yellow-tinged leaves signaled the end of the autumn raking. There would be no more blisters at the bases of our fingers, from wielding the bamboo rakes. However, there also would be no more running and jumping into mounds of leaves—a favorite pastime of ours that got us into much less trouble than leaping onto grandmother's sofa cushions.

Smoke also penetrated every layer of my warm clothing and burned my eyes on apple buttering day—the brisk autumn morning when we poured several bushels of apples, dried apple slices, and a few gallons of apple cider into a witch-sized cauldron and stirred and stirred and stirred to make the chocolate-brown apple spread that we used throughout the winter.

Left: Bologna hangs in the smokehouse for seasoning.

But smoke flavored much more than just an autumn day or two of my childhood. Our smokehouse sent curls of warm smoke skyward from late autumn through the winter and into early spring. It was the first aroma to greet me on winter mornings and the last to leave me as I drifted off to sleep after a goodnight kiss from my dad, whose hair, skin, and clothes seemed always to bear the smoke's perfume.

Once we could see our breath in the air, it was time to ready the smokehouse for the winter's worth of hams, bacon, bolognas, sausages, and dried beef that Dad and Uncle Emory would make for their customers at our butcher shop.

The first and worst step of the process, in my opinion, was our trip to the sawmill to gather hickory and apple wood sawdust. I dreaded those trips because we invariably arrived on dark, blustery evenings when haunting shadows and swirls of dust wreaked havoc with my already too-vivid imagination. As I held the burlap bags open and the men patiently shoveled them full, I couldn't help fidgeting and peering over my shoulder. Trouble lurked in those shadows, I thought, as I worried about being a hapless victim like those I'd read about in the Nancy Drew mysteries.

When the pickup truck's bed finally was filled with bags of sawdust, I was the first to pile into the truck's cab for the trip home. But there still was work to be done before the smokehouse fires were lit.

The arch cellar, an underground room next to our farmhouse and beneath my grandmother's potting shed, also had to be readied for its role in the meat-curing process. The cellar, with a 10-foot-high ceiling, was massive. Dug in the early 1700s to provide "refrigeration" for both summer and winter crops, it also served as a cool, curing room for hams and beef.

We descended the blue limestone slabs that were the stairs, carried the wooden shelves into

the sunlight and scrubbed them with water and salt. After the planks dried, they were taken back into the cellar and covered with the first of many batches of hams that were freshly rubbed with sugar, salt, and pepper, and remained in the cellar for a prescribed number of days.

When the time was up, the hams were plunged into a salt brine and then readied for the smokehouse. The big pieces of meat, 30 per batch, each had to be pierced with an oversized meat needle and run through with twine so that the twine could be used to tie the meats from the racks and rafters in the second-story of the smokehouse. Just trundling the hams in and out of the arch cellar and then carrying them up the narrow, twisting stairs in the smokehouse was hard work, considering that the men went through the process dozens of times a season.

The proportions used for the meat cures, as well as the hickory-to-apple blend of sawdust, were company secrets that Dad and Uncle Emory kept to themselves. But I know I looked forward to the day when they poured the blend of sawdust into the smokehouse fireplace and set a match to the mound after moistening it enough to keep it smoldering rather than bursting into flames. The second-floor room filled with smoke and became as black as night within minutes after we opened the second-floor chimney vent. But from that darkness emerged some of the most memorable meats of my childhood.

The bolognas, much like today's sweet and Lebanon bolognas, weren't ready for at least a month and a half. That's when they could first be cut and still hold their shape, and that's when they tasted best to me. My grandfather, on the other hand, liked bologna so smoked and so dried that it resembled super-thick beef jerky. He'd spend the better part of an hour chewing on just one chunk.

The first hams, still moist and mildly smoked, were ready in March or April—triggering the ham-for-Easter tradition in our part of the country. Some of the butcher shop customers liked them best this way. But others liked their hams heavily smoked and aged for a year or more, so Dad and Uncle Emory made sure these special hams were carefully marked with their owners' names and kept them until their customers came calling for them.

These hams, kissin' cousins to the country hams found in Kentucky, Tennessee, and North Carolina, are best-served in thin slices and small portions. Slice the meat thicker and it sometimes crumbles in the pan. To this day, there's probably no memory food I enjoy more than a center-cut slice of country ham, first simmered for a while in water and then cooked in milk for a while longer. The salty sweetness of the meat is wonderful with fresh greens, boiled potatoes, and corn on the cob.

In late spring, when the smoldering smokehouse fire was left to burn out, the building took on an entirely different look. The first floor, with its cool, concrete floor and few windows, became a cool summer's hideaway for me. On stifling days, I sometimes hid away for an hour or two to read a book or play with my dolls among the workbenches, wooden chairs, and crocks of preserved meats. At other times, I'd climb the stairs to look at the second floor, emptied of its hams, sides of bacon, and hunks of dried beef. When I switched on the light, I'd marvel at the ceiling's black-as-coal shine from thick layers of carbon that remained in it each year, and stare at the empty nails that still helped hold the memories of wonderful foods created in this room.

Left: Ham, sausage, and several types of bologna are among favorite meats enjoyed in my childhood home.

PRIME RIB ROAST — STANDING
SERVES 6

1 6-pound prime or top choice standing
  rib roast (with bone)
2 teaspoons salt
1 teaspoon pepper
1 teaspoon onion or garlic salt (optional)
Fresh herbs, finely chopped (if desired)
1 cup water

I prefer to use only salt and pepper when roasting such a fine cut of meat, but the preference is yours.

Moisten the roast with water to make sure the seasonings will stick. Place in roaster pan and add the water. Tent with foil and bake in preheated 300° F. oven for approx. 2 hours. To be sure the meat is cooked to your liking, use a meat thermometer. Remove the foil 35 minutes before serving to ensure even browning.

When serving only the eye of the roast, save the rest for barbecued ribs. Cut each rib apart and bake in shallow pan at 425° F. until crispy, adding barbecue sauce, or debone the meat for a wonderfully rich beef vegetable soup. After you remove the meat, return the bones, add some water, and simmer for an especially good broth. Cool, remove the fat, and refrigerate or freeze

HONEY-BAKED HAM

12 to 14 pound whole smoked, cured ham
4 cups water
1/2 cup honey
1/4 cup prepared mustard or 2
  Tablespoons dry mustard
Whole cloves (optional)
1/2 cup white or red wine (optional)
Fruit for garnish

Remove the rind from the cured ham and place bone side down in a roaster pan. Blend honey and mustard and pour over top of the ham. Add water to bottom of pan and tent with foil. If you are serving tableside, it looks nice if you score the fat into diamond shapes and center the diamonds with whole cloves. It also adds flavor to the ham and sauce. Bake in preheated 325° F. oven for approx. 3-1/2 hours or until tender.

If the ham is very salty, after baking for 2-1/2 hours, drain the water and add 2 cups of fresh water. Follow the directions for glazing and return the ham to the oven for another hour. If you do not want to serve it whole, debone and keep hot until serving. Deglaze the pan with wine, water, or fruit juice, and serve in sauce boat. Garnish as desired.

BASIC BEEF STOCK

2 to 3 pounds beef bones, untrimmed
Brownings from previous roast
6 cups water
1 Tablespoon salt (less if the meat
  was seasoned)
1 teaspoon black pepper
1 bay leaf
1 Tablespoon parsley, chopped
$^1/_4$ cup celery with leaves, chopped
$^1/_2$ teaspoon thyme, chopped
1 small onion, diced

In a large stockpot, place the meat, brownings, and water. Add the rest of the ingredients—the bones give an added flavor—and bring to a full boil. Reduce heat to medium and simmer for one to two hours. Remove from stove and cool. Skim the fat from the top and strain.

To clarify, whip 2 egg whites with a dash of vinegar until frothy. Whip into the broth and slowly bring to a boil. When it reaches the boiling point, remove from heat and strain through double layers of cheesecloth. Pour into containers suitable for freezing.

BRISKET OF BEEF STUFFING
SERVES 6

2 cups bread crumbs
2 stems celery, cleaned
$^1/_2$ red sweet bell pepper (if not
  available, use green)
$^1/_2$ green bell pepper
2 eggs
1 large carrot
1 teaspoon salt
$^1/_2$ teaspoon black pepper

Combine all the ingredients in food processor or blender until well blended. (If you do not have either piece of equipment, beat the eggs, chop the vegetables as fine as possible, and add the bread crumbs.) If the stuffing is too moist, add a bit more bread crumbs. If the stuffing does not fit in the brisket pocket, place in oiled baking dish and bake at 350° F. for approx. 35 minutes, placing it in the oven with the brisket. Serve on the side with the roast.

BRISKET OF BEEF
SERVES 6

This is not an expensive cut of meat, but served with style it becomes an elegant dish. Use your imagination; you are the one that creates "the dish."

2 to 2-1/2 pound beef brisket

Flavor is most important! It is best if roasted slowly and tented with foil. This method guarantees tenderness. It will nearly melt in your mouth. Removing the fat after roasting is best, insuring moisture and flavor. This is one cut of beef that needs to be served well done. The broth may be thickened with flour or cornstarch, adding extra herbs to complement the dish.

2 slices of bacon or 1 Tablespoon vegetable oil
3/4 teaspoon salt
1/2 teaspoon black pepper
Dash of favorite herbs if desired
1 to 2 cups water—this keeps the meat moist. It should be about 1/2 inch deep in roaster pan.

Place bacon in bottom of roaster pan or spread pan with vegetable oil. After seasoning the brisket, stuff or roll with fruit, jam, or your favorite bread or potato stuffing. Tie with string. Tent with foil. Bake in preheated oven at 325° F until meat thermometer registers "well-done," approximately three hours.

Beef Pie

2 Tablespoons butter
1 cup green bell pepper, chopped
1 cup onion, chopped
1-1/2 pounds lean ground beef
2 teaspoons salt
1 teaspoon seasoned salt
1/2 teaspoon black pepper
2-1/2 cups mushrooms, cleaned and sliced
1/2 cup celery, chopped
2-1/2 cups tomatoes, diced (canned are fine, if drained)
1/2 cup tomato ketchup
1 Tablespoon sugar
4 Tablespoons flour
1/2 cup cold water

Pastry:
2/3 cup vegetable shortening
1/3 cup butter
3 cups flour
1 teaspoon salt
3 eggs, beaten

To prepare the filling, melt the butter in a 3-quart saucepan or large heavy skillet. Sauté the green pepper and onions until the onions are golden. Add the beef, salts, and pepper. Brown lightly, breaking up the meat with a wooden spoon. Cook for about 10 minutes on medium heat until all traces of red have disappeared. Add the mushrooms, celery, tomatoes, ketchup, and sugar. Simmer for another 10 minutes. In a small bowl or a measuring cup, combine the flour and water, stirring until it is smooth. Gradually stir into the meat mixture. Cook a few minutes until thickened. Set aside.

To make pastry, cut or rub the shortening and butter into the flour and salt until crumbs are fine. Moisten crumbs with the beaten eggs, tossing gently with a fork until it forms a ball. Divide into 4 portions. Generously flour the pastry on top and bottom of each ball and roll the dough to fit the pans. Place 1 portion of rolled dough in each of 2 pans. Fill with the beef mixture and moisten edges with water. Top each pie with second crust, seal the edges, crimp, and cut a design in the center of each pie to allow steam to escape. Bake in a 9" pan in preheated 350° F. oven for 40 minutes or until light golden brown.

SECRETARY HAYES' BAKED CHOPS
SERVES 2 TO 3

This recipe could be described as one with layers of flavor, thanks to the initial shot of mint as well as the flavor-filled breading. I suggest using chops that are at least 1" thick.

Six lamb chops, cut 1" thick
1/2 teaspoon peppermint flavoring in 1/2 cup water, or 1/2 cup white crème de menthe
1 clove garlic, minced
1 Tablespoon seasoned herb salt
1 teaspoon black pepper
1/4 teaspoon fresh rosemary, finely chopped
1/2 teaspoon fresh dill, chopped
1 Tablespoon mint, chopped
1/2 teaspoon thyme, chopped (optional)
2 eggs, beaten until frothy
1 cup fresh bread crumbs
1/2 cup crushed corn flakes
Fresh herbs for garnish (mint, rosemary, parsley or thyme)

Note: For a special presentation, serve on a bed of peppery fresh watercress and edge the platter with red onion slices or if it is mid-summer, with slices of garden-ripened tomatoes.

Combine mint water or crème de menthe with minced garlic. Moisten the chops by dipping them into the mint-garlic mixture. Combine seasoned salt, pepper, rosemary, dill, mint, and thyme in a shallow pan and coat each chop with the herb mixture. Beat eggs until frothy and place in bowl. Combine fresh bread crumbs and crushed cereal in another bowl.

Dip each chop into the beaten egg and then into the crumb mixture until well-coated. Then place the chops in a greased baking pan. Roast in preheated 350° F. oven for approximately 15 minutes or until meat thermometer registers 145 degrees (medium rare). Baste with any remaining liquid and herb seasoning after the first five minutes. Turn chops periodically until they are golden brown. Remove and serve on a bed of watercress ringed with red onion or tomato slices.

Note: If you'd like chops to vary in their degree of doneness, vary the thickness of the chops used or shorten or lengthen the cooking times of the various chops.

SPECIAL MEAT LOAF
SERVES 4 TO 6

6 hard-cooked quail eggs or
  4 small chicken eggs
$1/2$ pound ground beef, lean
$1/2$ pound ground veal or turkey
2 eggs, beaten
1 Tablespoon chopped parsley
1 stem of celery, with leaves, diced
$1/2$ cup chopped tomatoes
$1/4$ cup diced onion
1 teaspoon salt
$1/2$ teaspoon pepper
$1/2$ cup milk
1 cup bread crumbs
Watercress or parsley for garnish

Cool eggs in cold water. Peel and set aside. In large bowl, mix all of the other ingredients (except eggs and garnish), blending thoroughly. Divide in two parts. Place first half of meat mixture in greased baking pan, pressing down with fingers to form into bottom half. Place the eggs end to end in the middle. Cover with the remaining half of the meat mixture, pressing the sides to seal. Optionally, top with $1/3$ cup freshly crumbled coarse bread crumbs. Bake in a preheated 375° F. oven for 1 hour. Garnish.

FRUITY STUFFED PORK CHOPS WITH WINE
SERVES 6

3 to 4 pounds thick-cut pork chops, each
   with a pocket cut in the meaty side
1 teaspoon salt
1 teaspoon pepper
1 teaspoon dry mustard
1 teaspoon brown sugar

For the filling:
6 slices of bacon, fried and drained
   when crisp
$1/2$ cup celery, chopped
$1/4$ cup onion, chopped
$1/4$ cup parsley, finely diced
$1/4$ cup honey or light brown sugar
4 cups fruit, drained and cut into bite-sized
   pieces. Use apples, seedless grapes,
   apricots, and peaches or any combination
   you prefer
1 cup saltine crackers, finely crushed
$1/2$ cup apple wine or golden sherry
   Lemon slices, sprigs of parsley and/or
   small button mushrooms that have been
   lightly sautéed in butter

Season outside of the chops lightly with
the mixture of salt, pepper, mustard, and
brown sugar.

To make the filling, cook six slices of bacon
in a large, deep skillet until the strips are
crisp. Remove from pan and drain the bacon.
Pour out all but two to three tablespoons of
bacon fat and add chopped celery and onion.
Cook on medium heat until onion and celery
are soft. Remove from heat and then add

the parsley, honey or light brown sugar, the
diced fruit, and the crushed cracker crumbs.
Stir to blend.

Loosely fill each chop with some of the filling. Place the filled chops in a large heavy
skillet coated with 2 Tablespoons butter or oil.
Quickly sear both sides of the chops. Then
reduce the heat and baste the chops with a
tablespoon or two of the apple wine or sherry.
Cover and cook for about three minutes per
side or until the filling is hot and the meat is
done. Remove chops from pan and add
remainder of the apple wine or sherry, to
deglaze the pan. Pour the resulting pan juices
into a gravy boat, or thicken them and serve
them as a wine gravy for the chops.

WIENER SCHNITZEL
SERVES 4 TO 6

2 pounds veal scallops, cut from leg,
   sliced $^1/_3$-inch thick
$^1/_2$ cup flour
1-$^1/_2$ teaspoons salt
$^1/_2$ teaspoon pepper
Pinch of dry mustard
Pinch of marjoram, or $^1/_2$ teaspoon
   fresh, chopped
2 large eggs, beaten
1 Tablespoon evaporated or whole milk
1 cup dry bread crumbs
$^1/_2$ cup saltine cracker crumbs (rolled fine)
$^1/_4$ cup vegetable oil
Lemon slices and fresh parsley sprigs
   for garnish

Score the edges of the scallops with a sharp
knife if there is any sinew around the edges.

Pound between sheets of wax paper until
approx. $^1/_4$-inch thick. Set aside. Combine the
dry ingredients and place in a plastic bag. Mix
the eggs and milk together in a shallow dish.

Take each scallop and dredge it in the bag of
dry ingredients, then dip it into the egg mixture, and finally dredge it in the bread/crack-
er crumb mixture. Pat to be sure the crumbs
will stick.

Heat oil in a large skillet over medium heat,
and fry until golden brown on each side, no
more than 3 minutes on each side. **Do not
overcook!** Serve on heated platter, garnishing
as desired.

BARBECUE SAUCE
YIELDS: ABOUT 2 CUPS

$^2/_3$ cup tomato paste or (6-ounce can)
1 Tablespoon Dijon mustard
$^1/_4$ cup honey or golden molasses
2 teaspoons dry mustard
$^1/_2$ cup light brown sugar
$^1/_2$ cup red wine
$^1/_2$ teaspoon salt
1 Tablespoon cider vinegar
1 teaspoon Worcestershire sauce
$^1/_2$ teaspoon onion or garlic
   powder (optional)
Dash or two of hot pepper sauce, according
   to taste.

In saucepan, combine all ingredients. Stir
over medium heat until blended. Simmer
on low heat for approx. 20 minutes, stirring
occasionally to prevent burning. This can be
stored in the refrigerator.

HOT SAUCE

1 cup ketchup
¹/₄ cup grated horseradish
1 Tablespoon lemon juice
1 teaspoon Worcestershire sauce
¹/₄ teaspoon salt
Dash of Tabasco or hot sauce

Blend all the ingredients thoroughly.

Refrigerate in a covered container. This sauce will keep in refrigerator for several weeks.

MUSHROOM SAUCE

YIELDS: ABOUT 1-1/2 CUPS

¹/₂ pound fresh mushrooms, cleaned and
   cut in half
¹/₄ cup minced onion
2 Tablespoons butter
2 Tablespoons flour
¹/₂ cup heavy cream (evaporated milk may
   be substituted)
¹/₂ cup sour cream
¹/₂ teaspoon salt
¹/₂ teaspoon white or black pepper

In heavy saucepan, sauté mushrooms and onion in butter until tender but not brown. Cover and simmer for 5 minutes over low heat. Slide mushrooms and onions to one side and stir in the flour. Blend and add cream, sour cream, salt and pepper. Heat but do not boil.

WINE-RAISIN SAUCE

2-¹/₂ cups dry red wine
1 cup sugar
2 Tablespoons prepared mustard
¹/₂ teaspoon salt
1 cup raisins
2 Tablespoons arrowroot
¹/₄ cup water

In 2-quart saucepan, add the wine, sugar, mustard, and salt. Blend and add raisins. Simmer on low heat for about 30 minutes. Dissolve the arrowroot in the water and stir into the sauce. Simmer until thickened, approx. 1 minute. Serve hot.

STREAM

*L*ike the huge sycamore leaves and gnarled seedpods we sailed in the stream, the water flowing through the meadow took us in many directions. No matter the time or season, it was a magnet drawing us together for all kinds of fun.

Sure the stream had certain "important" functions, like providing extra water for our garden and flower beds, chilling fresh milk before the farm had a modern refrigeration system, and providing drinking water for thirsty Holstein and Guernsey cattle grazing along its banks. But it was much, much more to me and my brother and cousins, and our Amish friends.

Sometimes, we did nothing more than stretch out on our stomachs on the lush green meadow grass, clipped first in the spring by the big mower on the tractor and then groomed for the rest of the season by the cattle. If there were no more leaves or seeds within reach, we'd drop twigs onto the water and watch them as if they were log rafts on a river. We'd toss pebbles into the stream and count the concentric rings that broke on the glassy surface. We'd trade tall tales about the "huge" fish our ancestors had caught in this stream. And sometimes, to scare each other, we talked about the trolls that I was certain lived under a bridge at the end of our property.

Left: An Amish family enjoys a holiday with a picnic and fishing at the stream.

If we were hungry, we loved having impromptu lunches by the stream. First, we ran to the farmhouse kitchen and helped ourselves to thick slices of homemade bread that we slathered with fresh butter. Then we hurried back to the meadow to pluck sprigs of watercress from the broad patches thriving along the water's edge. Although the cress became more pungent and peppery as it got older, and eventually bolted into delicate white flowers, we included it in our picnics all summer long. After dining, we'd spend some tranquil moments staring into crystal clear, quiet pools set off from the faster-running water by large, rounded rocks. We'd admire the surface reflections or contemplate our futures in nature's fluid looking glass.

But it wasn't long until these quiet moments were shattered. Sometimes, all it took was watching one of our Amish neighbors leap the stream on the way to our house to answer a call that had come in for them on our phone. Within a minute or two, one of my playmates would start a stream-jumping contest with a look and a dare. "Betcha you can't clear the stream over there," one would say to the other.

Like athletes in training, we'd take a couple of warm-up jumps before lining up for the heated competition. We kept leaping from bank to bank at ever-widening points of the streambed until someone unceremoniously fell short and landed in the water.

Our waterside gymnastics also included crossing the top of the concrete dam as if we were tightrope walkers. The shallow coating of water going over the dam made the moss that sparkled in the sun an emerald green and as slippery as ice. I must say, however, after a summer's worth of practice we all got very good at it. By August, I could go back and forth without getting even the hem of my dress wet.

Of course, we never missed a chance to get completely wet. Where the stream flowed into the Pequea Creek, there was a pool deep and wide enough to be our official swimming hole. On very hot days, thoughts of going for a cooling dip in the creek were like carrots in front of our noses. "If you finish weeding the garden…" "When we're done canning peaches…" "When all the watermelon rind has been made into pickles…" we were promised swims in the creek.

The story was the same on hot summer evenings. In the days before air conditioning, cavorting in the creek was one of the best ways to cool off. All of us would meet to take turns jumping off the diving board, playing some water tag, and floating in old, patched inner tubes from tractor tires. About the only time the water was off-limits was when the teenage boys in the neighborhood decided it was time for some skinny dipping and sunning. We couldn't make out much from the house, and darned if I could ever find binoculars. But I could really make them scatter by letting out some war whoops.

Adventures by the stream were so exciting that they made us feel like explorers on safaris. We sometimes ventured a few feet into a cave with an entrance that had been framed by rock walls. Adults told us those stones had been piled by the same Indians whose arrowheads turned up in the furrows when we plowed our fields in the spring.

We also summoned the courage for streamside snake hunts. We knew better than to go after any poisonous water snakes, including copperheads, but we never did see any of them.

Ordinary, spindly water snakes, none large enough to even make a skinny woman's belt, were fairly plentiful. They liked to sun themselves at the edge of the dam or on rocks that caught the afternoon rays. That's when we went into action. They were quick and clever so we had to create diversions. While one of us made some noises or tossed a rock on the bank, the other would sneak along in the shadows and then grab one of the slippery fellows who wriggled so much it was hard to measure it before it managed to squirm free.

We did better at catching and keeping fish. In fact, we imagined our catches of suckers

(bottom-feeding fish with large lips and mouths well-suited to sucking up minute bits of food from plants and rocks), sunfish, and the occasional trout were important contributions to family meals.

Although the adults managed to fill in with ample fish from the Susquehanna River, including shad, trout, and carp, as well as crabs, clams, and oysters from the Chesapeake, we worked hard to catch our share.

On the first day of trout season in the spring, some of the boys couldn't resist spending a few minutes fishing before walking to our one-room school. Of course, they'd usually forget themselves and the minutes stretched into nearly an hour before they'd come to their senses,

drop their fishing poles, and run to the school-house. When they slinked into their desks and offered feeble excuses to the scowling teacher, we all knew what they'd been doing. Wet, muddy shoes and the unmistakable earthy aromas of night crawlers and fish always gave them away.

It took sheer skill and experience to catch fish with our equipment. All of us had bamboo poles that already had been in our families, we believed, for several centuries. But that didn't stop us. We threaded them with fresh twine, and then tied a red and white bobber and a hook on each line. We dipped into our bait boxes (usually tin coffee cans filled with dirt and worms) and got busy.

We deftly cast our lines into the water and waited and waited. Our eyes stayed glued to the bobbers. The first time a red and white bobber skittered along the surface or popped under the water for a fleeting second or two, we knew a fish was taking a nibble of the bait. Then we waited for the fish to hit again, pulling that bobber under water. That's when we would set the hook by jerking the pole and pull our prey to shore.

After an afternoon of fishing, we congratulated ourselves on our day's catch and stood proudly as our parents oohed and ahhed over the fish we carried through the kitchen door. After the fish were scaled and gutted, we always enjoyed the pan-fried fillets for dinner the following night and never failed to campaign for new, store-bought fishing poles and fancy metal reels. "Just think how many fish we could catch," we'd say. Trouble was that after our parents finally obliged and bought us the new tackle, we didn't catch another fish until we went back to using our bamboo poles.

Previous Page: Teenage Amish girls wade in the stream close to their farm homes. Left: Watercress grows in the fresh water on the Groff farm now just as it did on my homestead.

TROUT, PAN FRIED — SERVED TABLESIDE
1 TROUT PER PERSON—IF LARGE, 1/2 PER PERSON

You may wish to use fillets of trout, deboned, etc. If you prefer using a fish from the stream, give my suggestion a try. Do not remove the head or fins. Clean properly, removing eyes, and season. Filling the fish with rice, lemon, or herbs will take more time, but will be impressive and tasty. Our late son John really enjoyed working in the restaurant kitchen with his fishing buddies after all the employees had gone home. The flavors had to be simple but great enough to make them want to come back again. He loved trying new recipes, but usually came back to the old standbys. I suppose children can only appreciate different spices and foods if they are encouraged to experiment with the flavors. But sometimes tried and true recipes still taste the best.

Trout, approx. $1/3$ pound per person, cleaned
Flour for dredging, approx. $1/2$ cup
2 eggs, lightly beaten with 1 teaspoon water or milk
Pecan breading (1 cup dry bread crumbs, 1 cup cornmeal, and 1 cup finely crushed pecans)
Butter or vegetable oil for frying, approx. 4 to 6 Tablespoons
$1/2$ teaspoon salt
$1/2$ teaspoon white pepper
$1/3$ cup white wine
1 Tablespoon lemon juice
Capers, lemon slices, and watercress for garnish

Dredge the trout in flour, dip in egg wash, and coat with pecan breading. Melt butter or oil in large frying pan. Lightly season fish with salt and pepper and brown on both sides until golden, about 3-5 minutes on each side. Sauté until the fish flakes at the thickest part. Remove onto heated platter and cover. Add wine and lemon juice to the brownings. Pour the sauce over the fish and garnish with capers, lemon slices, and watercress.

This recipe may be used for any fresh, whole fish. Chopped green scallions may be added when deglazing.

How to Fillet Trout

Have an extra plate for the bones. Gently lift the head and place a fork behind the gill and center backbone. Pull the head back toward the tail, and the whole backbone will come away from the fish, leaving the bottom fillet on the platter. Flip the fish over and lift out the spine with all the bones intact.

CREAM OF WATERCRESS SOUP
SERVES 6

3 Tablespoons butter
2 Tablespoons flour
1 teaspoon salt
$1/2$ teaspoon pepper
2 cups rich chicken broth
2 cups half-and-half (milk and cream)
1-$1/2$ cups finely chopped watercress
(cleaned and rinsed)
Sprigs of watercress and croutons for garnish

In a heavy 2-quart saucepan, melt the butter, blend in the flour, salt, and pepper on low heat. When well-mixed, whisk in the broth, milk, and watercress, stirring until soup is smooth, approx. 10 minutes. Garnish with sprigs of watercress and croutons.

CHARLIE'S FRIED OYSTERS
SERVES 6

24 large oysters, including the liquor
  or broth
1/2 cup fresh bread crumbs
1/2 cup cracker crumbs, crushed
1/2 teaspoon dry mustard
1/2 teaspoon pepper
1/2 teaspoon seafood seasoning
1 egg, lightly beaten
Oil for frying

Drain the oysters, saving the liquid for breading. Check the oysters for bits of shell. Pat the oysters with paper towels until dry. Dredge in the combination of crumbs, mustard, pepper, and seafood seasoning. Combine the oyster liquor and beaten egg. Dip the oysters in the egg mixture and roll them again in the remaining crumbs. Chill for at least 30 minutes. The breading sticks to the oysters better if they are chilled before frying. Pan or deep-fry in vegetable oil until golden. Serve at once with wedges of lemon or hot sauce.

SCALLOPED OYSTERS
SERVES 6

3 dozen oysters, medium size, freshly
   shucked with their liquor
1 cup fresh bread crumbs, divided
$1/2$ teaspoon salt
$1/2$ teaspoon pepper
1 Tablespoon lemon juice
$1/2$ cup butter, melted
2 cups small oyster crackers
1 egg, lightly beaten
1 cup cream, half-and-half, or milk
Garnish with a dash of paprika or
   seafood seasoning

Always check the oysters for tiny bits of
shell. In a 1-$1/2$ quart baking dish, butter and
sprinkle with $1/4$ cup bread crumbs. Add half
the oysters, and half of the salt, pepper,
lemon juice, and butter. Layer with oyster liquid and crackers. Combine the beaten egg
and cream or milk. Pour over the above. Add
remaining oysters, seasonings, butter, and
sprinkle with the remaining crumbs. Garnish
with seasoning and bake in preheated 375° F.
oven for 35 minutes.

SHAD ROE

3 pair of shad roe
1/3 cup flour
1/4 teaspoon salt
1/2 teaspoon white pepper (black may
   be substituted)
6 slices smoked bacon
2 lemons, cut in wedges
Watercress or spinach for base on platter

Place flour, salt, and pepper in paper or plastic bag. Gently shake each roe until completely covered. Separate each pair by removing the fiber that holds them together, being careful not to pierce the thin membrane covering the roe.

In heavy skillet, place the bacon and then the roe, and slowly heat until the bacon begins to curl. Partially cover with lid or mesh spatter-proof lid, as roe has a tendency to splatter. On medium heat, fry until golden brown on each side. When turning them over, be very gentle—they are so delicate and look beautiful if kept intact.

Serve on a bed of watercress, spinach, or delicate greens with lemon wedges around the roe. Remove the bacon, pat dry with paper towels, and crumble it on top of roe or leave strips whole. An herb vinegar also is a pleasant accompaniment.

CRISPY FILLETS OF FISH
SERVES 6

6 fillets of flounder or other mild
  boneless fish
$1/2$ to $3/4$ cup flour—amount depends on
  size of fillets
$1/2$ teaspoon salt
$1/2$ teaspoon white pepper
Egg wash—2 large eggs lightly beaten with
  1 Tablespoon water
1-$1/2$ cups potato or corn chips,
  finely crushed
4 Tablespoons vegetable oil or margarine
  3 to 4 Tablespoons of butter or 2
  Tablespoons of olive oil
Fresh parsley
Lemon, thinly sliced, half for garnish and
  half that may be placed around fish for
  the final minutes of cooking

Rinse fillets and pat dry with paper towels. Place flour, salt, and pepper in a large plate or platter. Add your favorite herbs to the mixture to make it your specialty. Be careful not to overpower the delicate flavor of the fish with herbs that are too strong. In a deep dish or pan, pour the egg wash or lightly beat it in the pan. Place the crushed chips in another pan. Now you're ready! Dip each fillet into the flour mixture, then the egg wash, and finally the crushed chips. Pat firmly to keep all the breading intact. If time allows, refrigerate for about 30 minutes. In large skillet, heat oil on medium heat, browning fillets until golden on each side. Reduce heat to low, add butter, a few lemon slices, and simmer for a few minutes or until it flakes when you insert a fork or knife into the thickest part. Serve on heated platter. Garnish with fresh parsley and thinly sliced lemons.

Variation: Perch and whiting are great prepared this way. Add some chopped green onions, a bit of seafood seasoning, capers, or garnish with fresh watercress and fresh salsa for a delightful change. I like sautéed bananas, pineapple, kiwi, and toasted almonds in butter and fruit schnapps as a topping when I want an elegant presentation. Use your imagination.

BAKED TILAPIA

SERVES 4 TO 6

¹/₄ cup butter
¹/₂ cup bread crumbs
¹/₂ teaspoon Old Savannah Seasoning
   (Old Bay may be substituted)
1-¹/₂ pounds fresh tilapia (haddock or cod
   may be substituted)
¹/₃ cup milk
³/₄ teaspoon salt
¹/₂ teaspoon white pepper
¹/₂ cup white wine

Generously spread butter in bottom of

9″ x 13″ baking dish. Sprinkle crumbs and seasoning evenly. Dip fish in milk and place on crumbs. Add salt, white pepper, and wine.

¹/₄ cup melted butter
¹/₂ cup bread crumbs

Combine butter and crumbs and sprinkle on top of fish

Bake in preheated 350° F. oven for 15 minutes or until fish flakes when pierced with a fork. Garnish with lemon slices and parsley or fresh watercress.

CLAM AND CORN PIE

4 cups fresh corn, cut off the cob
¹/₂ cup raw clams or canned minced clams
4 eggs, lightly beaten
1 teaspoon salt
2 teaspoons sugar
Freshly ground pepper to taste
2 tablespoons flour
¹/₂ cup melted butter
9-inch unbaked pie shell, plus enough
   pastry for a top crust (recipe on
   page 117)

Combine the corn, clams, eggs, salt, sugar, pepper, flour, and butter. Pour into the pie shell. Cover with the top crust, making a vent for the steam to escape. Bake in a 350° F. oven for 1 hour.

DAIRY

✦◆✦◆✦◆✦◆✦◆✦

*T*wo rounded scoops of vanilla ice cream tottering on a tall sugar cone were all the proof I needed that my life on the farm was as rich as the cream that rose to the top of old-fashioned glass milk bottles.

Ice cream was the year-round treat that couldn't be licked, not by a multi-tiered cake or even a handful of chocolate chip cookies. Whenever Uncle Emory began icing the 8-quart freezer, adding sea salt and pouring in the mixture of eggs, cream, and sugar, he was guaranteed an audience that didn't disperse until everyone had a cone or dish of his latest creation. Most times, he produced great tasting vanilla ice cream that was at its best when covered with homemade chocolate fudge sauce. Occasionally, he added Grape-Nuts cereal to the mix for a little crunch. But his best variations, by far, were made during the summer, when he added fresh-picked strawberries, red or black raspberries, or sugar-sweet golden peaches to the ice cream a few minutes before he stopped turning the crank.

Left: Early in the morning, Amish family members go to the barn to help with the milking. *Pages 78–79:* Dairy cows and mules on a Lancaster County farm graze in the grass and mustard flowers.

On steamy summer evenings when we children didn't even feel like chasing fireflies' twinkling lights, we needed no coaxing to lift our spoons and make Uncle Emory's ice cream vanish. But we were just as anxious for ice cream when snow and ice blanketed the land. No one ever refused ice cream, even when we knew it would surely make us shiver for the rest of the evening.

Although I appreciated milk most in its frozen form, my mother and aunt had many ways to use pitcher after pitcher of milk that poured into their kitchens.

A mug of warm milk, with a little salt and

pepper and topped by a piece of buttered toast was our version of chicken soup. It might not have cured anything, but it was a comforting sign that we were getting better.

When we were feeling good, we downed homemade cheeses, casseroles, soups, puddings, and custards and pies whose key ingredient was the milk from our herd of 30 black-and-white Holsteins. Although Holstein milk isn't as filled with cream as that from golden Guernseys, it is more plentiful. With proper feeding and care, the cows produced milk rich enough to satisfy our family of particular cooks as well as the commercial dairy that based the

price paid for the milk on the amount of cream it contained.

Milking the herd was on a fixed schedule, at 5:30 a.m. and 5:30 p.m., because it was essential to insuring steady milk production from the cows. Milking was the first task of the day, done before anyone saw a sunny-side-up egg or a strip of bacon. And no matter what else was scheduled for evening, from school dances to ice-skating or sledding parties, the cows came first. Although the men did most of the morning milking, we all pitched in when needed or when there was a cow the men couldn't handle.

Evening milking began when one of us children was sent to the pasture to summon the cows, using a special tone and call that sounded like, "Sook, sook, sook." I don't know who first used the call, but it was one the cows would answer. When they heard it, they fell in behind the lead cow and paraded like a precision marching unit, single-file, to the barn. But even calling them was more ritual than necessity. Their body clocks were amazingly accurate and often they'd begin their march to the barn on their own.

Milking the cows was more difficult than getting them into the barn. Jezebel, in particular, was the meanest milker I remember. She'd look at you sweetly until you got close enough to kick, and then she'd let one of her hooves fly. The men struggled with her every day, until the time my mother first looked her squarely in the eye and faced her down. From that day onwards, Jezebel was my mother's pet project. The ritual was the same every day. Mother would don her milking coat, tie a bandanna over her hair and walk along the stalls until she reached Jezebel's. Then, she'd stroke Jezebel's muzzle gently and say, in a whisper, "Jezebel, I'm going to milk you." With that, the cow would shake her head as if nodding OK, and then busy herself chomping on some fodder while mother went about filling the milk pail.

Milking any cow quickly and efficiently, but gently, requires some patience. But once learned, it's about as automatic as working a car's stick shift. A favorite cow would get a few gentle strokes on her sides first, or a pat on the nose. Then, we'd sometimes hum or whistle or even sing in harmony to soothe our charges while tugging on their teats to get every last drop of milk. Occasionally, however, we young ones strayed a bit from the original purpose of milking.

One evening, I remember boasting about how quickly I was going to be finished with my row of "easy milkers," while my brother and the hired hand were struggling to milk some of the more stubborn cows in the herd. I kept up the banter until my brother decided to silence me by firing a stream of milk my way. He nailed me squarely on the forehead. Some even flew into my mouth.

I sputtered indignantly as the milk dripped off my face and onto my frock. That fired me up and a milk battle began in earnest. I took aim and made some direct hits myself. I think I was actually winning the skirmish handily when Dad walked into the barn and spotted us. He was not amused. The hired hand got a scolding and we missed out on an evening visit to the swimming hole. We were too busy scrubbing the barn. The only real winner of the fight was the barn cat who willingly licked up a hearty share of the spilled milk.

I can't imagine that Dad never engaged in similar battles as a boy, but he definitely dealt with us in true, gruff, grown-up style. I suppose he was annoyed at the milk we wasted, which could have been sold or, in my mother's and aunt's hands, could have been turned into some fabulous foods.

Whenever the cows were being milked, we poured pail after pail of milk into spotless stainless steel milk cans that chilled in a pool of icy-cold spring water until we hauled them to the train depot via horse and buggy or, in later years, until the dairy's tanker truck arrived to pick up the milk.

Each day, however, a gallon was reserved for

the family's use. We got one quart of milk up-home at our house, while the other three quarts went to the farm kitchen in my grandparents' house, where the bulk of the heavy cooking was done. Every few days, the men also skimmed off a little extra cream for whipping into special treats.

Milk poured from the pitchers when it was time to make cool summer fruit soups and for oyster stew as well as stick-to-your-ribs winter soups like chunky cream of potato, peppery cream of watercress, bacon-flecked corn chowder, and even smoky country ham and bean soup. Thick. Hearty. So full of meat and vegetables that they were served on the old white ironstone dinner plates with slightly sunken centers, rather than in ordinary soup bowls.

But soups weren't on the menu as often as we have them today, because they weren't appreciated. They were considered a sign of hard times. If we dared serve more than one soup-centered meal a week, the men began asking "Is there something we should know?" or "What have we done wrong to deserve this?"

No one complained, however, when the milk was turned into cheese. We loved cottage cheese (to be served with apple butter), pungent "cup cheese" that oozed with the essence of barnyard in every spoonful, ball cheese, and egg cheese, which was my favorite. Its consistency was similar to the texture of light, creamy ricotta cheese.

To make the egg cheese, which we usually spread on bread along with a drizzling of honey or mild molasses, regular milk is mixed with eggs, buttermilk, salt, and sugar. The ingredients then are heated in a saucepan until the curds separate from the whey. The curds are lifted from the pan and gently placed in heart-shaped, perfo-

rated tin molds to firm up and hold the shape of the molds. Then the cheese is ready to be unmolded and plated so that it's ready for spreading. I still love snacking on it, and often serve it at parties as an easy *hors d'oeuvre*.

Cheeses of all kinds, including Swiss and cheddar, were readily available in Lancaster County, where farmers got into the habit of making it when prices for liquid milk were down. It also was at the heart of one of my earliest culinary specialties—macaroni and cheese. When I joined the 4-H club, the two recipes I recreated for my family were tuna noodle casserole and macaroni and cheese. Unfortunately, the tuna noodle casserole was so bad that my father excused himself from our table and went down to the farm kitchen for a meat-and-potatoes meal. The macaroni and cheese, however, was a great success. In fact, every time I wanted to make a meal, the family insisted on macaroni and cheese. Only years later did I learn that they requested it for fear I'd try making that tuna-noodle casserole again.

Mother's baked egg custard (like crème brulee minus the crisp brown-sugar topping) was sprinkled with a little brown sugar or cinnamon just before it was placed in a water bath and baked in the oven. But friends we knew sometimes got a little fancier with it. They sprinkled some black or red raspberries or blueberries on the top of the custard before baking it, to give it a little more color and flavor.

Extra milk could become any number of puddings or pie fillings, including vanilla, chocolate, tapioca, rice, or cornstarch. Rice pudding, which slow-cooked for hours in a heavy pot on the back of the stove, teased us with its aroma long before the mixture of milk, rice, butter, and vanilla thickened enough to be served. Cornstarch pudding could be eaten warm or cold and sometimes was topped with a little chocolate syrup. But it also was the most popular filling I used in the 25-cent cream puffs I made and contributed to school bake sales.

Cracker pudding, made from crushed saltine

crackers, coconut, sugar, vanilla, and our farm's milk and fresh eggs, is one of the more unusual dairy-based desserts we made. When we were entertaining, Mother went through the added step of topping it with a cloud-like layer of meringue that was baked just long enough to turn the meringue a light golden brown. Baked in a glass Pyrex bowl, the cracker pudding always was placed in a silver-plated server before being placed on the table.

Although it sounds like a rather humble dessert, cracker pudding has been so popular with guests at Groff's Farm Restaurant that it has been served every day we have been open in the last 40-some years. In all that time, my husband and I found only one more use for the milk from our own cows that rivaled the treats we produced on the farm—sending it off to nearby Hershey to become milk chocolate Hershey bars and Kisses.

Previous page: A heart-shaped, tin mold I use for making egg cheese. *Left:* An Amish girl gives milk to a calf recently weaned from its mother.

BASICS

CHEESE SAUCE
YIELDS: ABOUT 4 CUPS

2 Tablespoons butter
2 Tablespoons flour
3 cups chicken stock
1 Tablespoon minced onion
1 Tablespoon minced celery
$^1/_2$ teaspoon minced fresh basil
  (if dried, $^1/_4$ teaspoon)
2 Tablespoons cornstarch
$^1/_2$ cup milk

10 ounces yellow mild cheddar cheese, grated
6 ounces American cheese, grated

In large saucepan, melt the butter on low heat. Slowly stir in the flour until smooth. Whisk in the chicken stock, onion, celery, and basil. Simmer for 20 minutes. Combine the cornstarch with the milk and add to the broth to thicken. Add cheeses and stir until smooth.

WHIPPED CREAM
YIELDS: AT LEAST 2 CUPS

Chill the bowl and beaters in freezer before you begin.

1 cup heavy cream
2 Tablespoons granulated sugar
$^1/_2$ teaspoon vanilla extract

Pour cream into large, chilled mixing bowl. Beat with an electric mixer on medium-high speed until it forms soft peaks, about 2 minutes. Gradually add the sugar and vanilla and continue beating until it forms firm peaks.

CHOCOLATE SAUCE

$^1/_2$ cup sugar
2 Tablespoons flour
$^1/_8$ teaspoon salt
1 cup water
1 square (2 ounces) chocolate
$^1/_4$ teaspoon vanilla extract

In heavy saucepan, thoroughly mix the sugar, flour, and salt. Gradually add the water,

stirring to make a smooth sauce. Add the chocolate and bring to a boil over medium heat. Reduce heat and simmer approx. 2 minutes until the chocolate is melted. Remove from heat and add vanilla. If sauce becomes too thick, add a little hot water, and stir until smooth. This keeps well for at least a week in the refrigerator if properly sealed.

MACARONI AND CHEESE CASSEROLE
SERVES 6

8 cups water
2 cups (8 ounces) macaroni or other pasta
Pinch of saffron, crushed
1/2 teaspoon salt
1 Tablespoon butter or olive oil
1/2 cup grated Velveeta cheese
1/2 cup grated cheddar cheese
1/2 cup grated white American cheese
1/2 teaspoon salt
1/2 teaspoon white pepper
2 cups milk
Buttered crumbs
Dash of paprika
Parsley and sliced olives for garnish

In large pot, bring water to a boil. Add macaroni, saffron, salt, and butter or oil, and boil uncovered, on medium heat, until tender, approx. 12 minutes. Drain and place in a large mixing bowl. Stir in the cheeses, salt, pepper, and milk until well blended. Pour into buttered two-quart baking dish, cover with buttered crumbs, and bake in preheated 350° F. oven for approx. 30 minutes or until golden brown on top. Remove and garnish with a bit of paprika, parsley, and sliced olives.
This recipe is great for freezing in individual or full portions.

COCONUT CREAM PIE

1 baked pie shell
2 cups milk, divided
2/3 cup sugar
1/2 teaspoon salt
3 Tablespoons cornstarch
2 eggs, separated
1-1/2 Tablespoons butter
1 teaspoon vanilla
1-1/4 cups shredded coconut, divided

Meringue:
A pinch of cream of tartar
2 egg whites
4 Tablespoons sugar

Scald 1-1/2 cups milk in top of a double boiler. Combine the 2/3-cup sugar, salt, and cornstarch with the remaining 1/2-cup milk, mixing into a smooth paste. Add to the hot milk and cook, stirring until thickened. In a small bowl, beat the egg yolks, add a small amount of the hot milk mixture, and blend. Pour into the hot milk mixture and cook on low heat for 2 minutes. Remove from heat and mix in the butter, vanilla, and 3/4 cup of the coconut. Cool and pour into the pie shell.

Beat the egg whites with the cream of tartar until they hold soft peaks. Gradually beat in the 4 Tablespoons of sugar until it is stiff and glossy. Cover the pie filling with meringue, making sure you spread meringue to cover and touch the edges of the pie shell. Sprinkle the remaining 1/2 cup of coconut over the meringue. Bake in preheated 350° F. oven for 5 minutes or until meringue is a delicate golden color.

CRACKER PUDDING
SERVES 6

1 quart milk
2 eggs, separated
²/₃ cup sugar
2 cups (1 package) broken saltine crackers
   (not rolled into crumbs)
1 cup grated coconut, fine or medium shred
1 teaspoon vanilla extract

¹/₂ recipe of Great Meringue (optional) (See recipe on page 47)

In a heavy 3-quart pot, heat the milk almost to the boiling point. In a bowl, beat the egg yolks and sugar until frothy and light. Gradually add to the hot milk. Reduce heat to medium. Crumble the crackers into the hot milk, stirring constantly until the mixture comes to a boil. Add the coconut and stir until the pudding bubbles thickly or heavily. Remove from the heat and add the vanilla. Beat the egg whites until stiff but not dry. Fold into pudding, return to stove, and simmer on low for a few minutes. Pour into serving dish and top with extra meringue, toasted under the broiler until golden, if desired. The meringue gives it an elegant touch.

RICE PUDDING
SERVES 6

Why is this pudding so creamy? Natural rice, cooked slowly, is the answer. A crock pot is one way of cooking it, although a double boiler will work if you can control the heat. Do not let the rice become dry.

1 cup long-grain rice
2 cups water
1 teaspoon salt, divided
6 cups milk
1/2 cup butter or margarine
1/4 cup granulated sugar
2 large eggs, beaten
1 teaspoon vanilla extract

In medium saucepan, add rice, water, and 1/2 teaspoon salt. Boil over medium heat for 15 minutes. Drain. In large heavy saucepan or on top of double boiler (over simmering water), heat the milk, butter, and remaining salt until butter melts. Add the rice and simmer over low heat, slightly covered, for 1-1/2 hours, stirring often to prevent sticking.

Combine sugar and beaten eggs with rice, mixing until blended. Simmer until thickened but not boiling, approx. 15 minutes. Remove from heat and add vanilla.* Serve warm or chilled with fruit or jam topping.

Extras: * Zest of lemon and 1 Tablespoon lemon juice, 1 cup raisins and nuts or several dashes of cinnamon.

Honey or Maple Whipped Cream

When making whipped cream (page 85), add 1/4 cup honey or pure maple syrup and pinch of salt to the cream. Omit the sugar and vanilla.

EGG CHEESE
SERVES 6 OR MORE

Lancaster County, Pennsylvania, homemakers pride themselves on the quality and texture of this delicate cheese. Old molds are regarded as heirlooms, although artisans now are reproducing them with success. Knowing when to drain, how to unmold, and ways to present are important to serving this heritage food. Naturally–woven baskets, small and with different shapes and sizes, are great for this purpose. Remove handles, scrub, rinse, and you're ready. A pottery or porcelain *Coeur a la creme* mold will be fine, too.

4 cups milk
3 eggs, beaten until fluffy
1 cup buttermilk
$1/2$ teaspoon salt
1 teaspoon sugar
Dash of nutmeg
Chopped herbs, chives, parsley, etc.
   (optional)
Golden molasses, honey, fresh berries
   or jam
Bread squares, rounds or slices

Heat milk in large saucepan over medium heat until warm—do not boil. Combine beaten eggs, buttermilk, salt, and sugar. Slowly add to milk, stirring constantly. Cover with lid, adjust heat to low, simmering for a few minutes. Stir occasionally, being careful to prevent sticking to the bottom of pan.

Remove the lid and watch carefully for the curds (cheese) and whey to separate. The liquid (whey) turns from cloudy to clear. Add the chopped herbs, if desired, as you see the liquid become clear. Place molds on tray. Immediately, using a slotted spoon, transfer the curds lightly into the molds. Do not pour to drain or the cheese will be solid in texture.

Cool until all liquid is drained, approx. 30 minutes. Unmold cheese onto presentation plates. Chill and garnish. Serve with breads, honey, fruits, etc.

CARAMEL PUDDING
SERVES 6

2 Tablespoons butter
1 cup light brown sugar
$1/2$ teaspoon salt
3 cups milk, divided
1 Tablespoon flour
2-$1/2$ Tablespoons cornstarch
3 eggs, lightly beaten
1 teaspoon vanilla
Whipped cream
Chocolate shavings

Important: Follow instructions in order given.

Melt butter in a heavy skillet or deep saucepan. Add the brown sugar and salt, stirring constantly over medium heat until it caramelizes, approx. 5 minutes - do not burn. Remove from stove and cool for a short time. Slowly mix in 2 cups of milk until smooth. Return to stove and heat thoroughly, stirring constantly.

In a separate bowl, mix remaining cup of milk with flour and cornstarch, making a smooth paste. Blend with the mixture in the saucepan and return to stove. Reduce heat to low, stirring until thickened and smooth. Remove and place 1 cup of hot pudding into a bowl.

Gradually whip the beaten eggs into mixture and return to the pudding, combining all. Return to stove, on low and heat for approx. 2 minutes. Do not boil. Remove from stove, add the vanilla, and pour into serving dish.

Garnish with whipped cream and chocolate shavings.

ICE CREAM – BASIC VANILLA

YIELDS: 4 QUARTS

4 large eggs
2-2/3 cups sugar or 1 cup honey and
  1 cup sugar
1/3 teaspoon salt
2 13-ounce cans evaporated milk
1-1/2 cups heavy cream
1 cup milk
1 Tablespoon vanilla extract
1 to 1-1/2 cups crushed fruit, berries, or
  chocolate chips, cookies, etc. (optional).
  A dash of nutmeg or a few drops of lemon
  extract enhance many of the fruit flavors.

In a large mixing bowl, cream the eggs, sugar, and salt until fluffy. Stir in the evaporated milk, cream, milk, and flavoring (plus any fruit or chips you choose to add). Pour into the freezer can of a 4-quart ice cream freezer and cover with lid. Pack with crushed ice and rock salt, layered. Using rock salt, or ice cream salt, saves time while turning. If it is an electric mixer, rock salt still works better than iodized salt. Add crushed ice as it melts, keeping ice right up to the top of the outside of the freezer. Take care that the salt-ice mixture does not get into the ice cream can. Follow directions with freezer for removing the ice cream.

BAKERY

The dust never settled in our farmhouse kitchen because it came from the flour in our mixing bowls. Each day, we'd scoop out some more flour from the barrel to make the bread we needed, as well as to bake pies, cakes, sweet breads, and cookies that helped us tell family and friends how much we cared about them.

Although baking was as much a part of our routine as weeding the garden, washing clothes, or cooking dinner, it wasn't like the other tasks. Turning the wheat we grew on our land into bread and baked goods was part wonder and part magic, a miracle in which we had just a small hand.

Mondays and Thursdays were the days my mother, aunt, and I routinely made 14 loaves of white and whole wheat bread. Instead of standard loaf pans, ours were 10-inch rounds, yielding loaves the size of soccer balls. But they'd disappear by the time the next baking day rolled around because we were baking for three families plus hired hands or about 14 people.

It seemed as if we always were carving away at the loaves. We toasted slices for breakfast that were slid under fried eggs, dipped into the yolks of sunny-side up eggs, or covered with cream-dried beef or sausage gravy. Some of the hired hands could use chunks or slices of bread to "wipe their plates" so clean of any leftover egg yolk, crusty home fries, or bits of bacon that they almost looked washed when we collected them. But we children were discouraged from doing the same, and had to be content topping our toast with butter, jelly, honey, or apple butter spread as thick as the icing on a cake.

At our noon meal, the main one of the day, bread was as important as a side dish and was spread with butter unless it was needed for a more important role, like for gravy bread. Sometimes it also made it to the table in more than one form, like a savory bread stuffing or a sweet bread pudding.

Left: Wheat is harvested on a Lancaster County farm.

In the evening, there was more bread for meaty sandwiches piled high with Lebanon bologna, ham, or leftover chicken, as well as more delicate creations like egg or ham salad and sandwiches made with nothing more than sliced radishes, watercress, or fresh leaf lettuce and butter. During hot spells, we'd make fruit soups by layering broken or cubed bread, fresh berries or sliced peaches and sweetened milk.

Bread also filled in the cracks when my brother, cousins, and I needed snacks. When a rounded loaf was cut in half and placed with the cut sides down on the board, I always asked for the nicely browned heel or top crust and would eat it plain because I loved that buttery, nutty flavor. But if I got stuck with a center slice, I had to butter it to get it down. A teaspoon or two of jelly also helped the bread go down.

Left: The grains used for bread flour were grown on my childhood farm.

BASICS

CARAMEL ICING

¹/₂ cup butter
1 cup light brown sugar, lightly packed
¹/₄ cup evaporated milk or ¹/₃ cup
  heavy cream
Pinch of salt
2 cups (or 1 pound) confectioners' sugar
¹/₂ teaspoon vanilla extract

In a large saucepan, melt the butter, add the brown sugar, and bring to a boil over medium heat. Reduce heat to medium-low for 2 minutes, <u>stirring constantly</u>. Remove from heat and stir while adding the milk and salt. Return to the stove and bring to a full boil. Remove from heat and let cool until lukewarm. In mixing bowl, gradually beat in the confectioners' sugar and vanilla, beating until the icing is smooth enough to spread.

**Double this recipe if you are making a three or four layer cake.

BUTTER CREAM FROSTING

¹/₂ cup butter or ¹/₄ cup butter and
  ¹/₄ cup cream cheese
2 Tablespoons cream or half-and-half
1 pound confectioners' sugar
Pinch of salt
¹/₂ teaspoon vanilla extract

In a large mixing bowl, blend all the ingredients. Beat until light and fluffy. Spread on cake.

**You will need to double this recipe if you are making a high layer cake.

BASIC WHITE BREAD

YIELDS: 3 LOAVES, 5″ X 11″ EACH

2 cups scalded milk
3 Tablespoons sugar
1-1/4 Tablespoons salt
3 Tablespoons butter
2 packages dry granular yeast
1/4 cup lukewarm water (110° F.)
7 cups flour, sifted (stone-ground flour
   is great, too)
Melted butter

Cool the milk to lukewarm, and add the sugar, salt, and butter. Let the yeast proof by dissolving in lukewarm water—it should form tiny bubbles on the surface, showing it is active. Add yeast mixture to the milk. Combine with the flour and mix thoroughly. Knead vigorously on a lightly floured surface or in an electric mixer with a dough hook, until the dough is smooth and elastic to the touch. Put the dough in a greased bowl, turning it so it is oily on all sides. Cover with a damp cloth and let it rise in a warm, draft-free spot until double in bulk. Cut or punch down and knead a bit more. Divide the dough into 3 parts, shaping each into a smooth loaf. Place in greased loaf pans. Cover with a cloth. Let the dough rise in a warm place until doubled in bulk. Bake in a preheated 350° F. oven for 45 minutes or until the bread pulls away from the sides of pan. Brush the top of the loaves with melted butter.

BASIC WHOLE WHEAT BREAD

YIELDS: 3 LOAVES, 5″ X 11″ EACH

Use Basic White Bread recipe, substituting whole wheat flour for 1/2 of the white flour. Add 1/4 cup honey to the milk mixture.

OLD FASHIONED CHOCOLATE CAKE

MAKES ONE 9-BY-13 INCH CAKE
OR TWO 9-INCH ROUND LAYERS

2 cups light brown sugar, lightly packed
1/2 cup butter, margarine, or shortening
2 large eggs
3/4 cup buttermilk
1/2 cup unsweetened cocoa
1/2 cup coffee, hot and strong
1 teaspoon baking soda
1 teaspoon cider vinegar
1/2 teaspoon salt
1 teaspoon vanilla extract
2-1/2 cups sifted flour

Cream the sugar and butter together in a large mixing bowl until fluffy. Add the eggs one at a time, beat a minute, and then add the buttermilk. Put cocoa in a small bowl and add the coffee, stirring or using a whisk to prevent lumping. Add to the creamed mixture, blending well. Put baking soda in a small bowl and moisten with vinegar. Add to creamed mixture. Blend in the salt and vanilla. Gradually add the flour, beating until smooth. Pour batter into greased and floured 9-by-13-inch cake pan or two 9-inch round layer pans. Bake in preheated 350° F. oven for 45 minutes or until a toothpick inserted in the center of cake comes out clean. Cool and frost with your favorite icing. I prefer Caramel Icing or Butter Cream Frosting (see recipes on page 97).

WHITE MOUNTAIN CAKE

MAKES ONE 9-BY-13 INCH CAKE
OR TWO 9-INCH ROUND LAYERS

2/3 cup shortening
1-1/2 cups sugar
2-1/2 cups flour, sifted
1/2 teaspoon salt
3-1/2 teaspoons baking powder
3/4 cup milk
1 teaspoon vanilla
4 large egg whites
Your favorite frosting

In large mixing bowl, cream the shortening. Gradually add the sugar, beating until light and fluffy. In another large bowl, sift the sifted flour, salt, and baking powder together. Add the dry ingredients to the creamed mixture alternately with the milk and vanilla, beating thoroughly after each addition. In a smaller bowl, beat the egg whites until stiff and gently fold into the cake batter. Pour into two greased 9-inch layer cake pans. Bake in preheated 350° F. oven for approx. 30 minutes or until a toothpick inserted in the center of cake comes out clean. Cool and frost with your favorite icing.

CRUMB CAKE

4 cups flour
3/4 cup butter or margarine
2-1/2 cups brown sugar
1 teaspoon cinnamon
1/2 teaspoon ground cloves
1/2 teaspoon ground nutmeg
2 teaspoons baking soda
1-1/2 cups buttermilk
1 teaspoon vanilla

Blend the flour, butter or margarine, sugar, and spices with a pastry blender or hands until it makes fine crumbs. Keep 1-1/2 cups of crumbs for topping. Dissolve baking soda in the buttermilk and mix with remaining crumbs until blended. Pour into oiled or buttered pans, topping with reserved crumbs. Bake in preheated 350° F. oven for 35 to 40 minutes, depending on size and depth of pans. When touched lightly, the cake should spring back. Serve warm and top with any fresh or canned fruit and you'll have a real treat that's nice enough to serve to guests.

Apricot-Nut Bread

1 recipe of Basic Sweet Dough – Page 131
1/3 cup melted butter or margarine
1/4 cup cinnamon/sugar (half and half)
1/2 cup dried apricots, chopped
1/2 cup nuts—pecans, walnuts, etc.

On floured surface, roll the dough into a large rectangle. With pastry brush, spread the melted butter over dough, covering completely. Sprinkle with cinnamon sugar mixture, apricots, and nuts. Roll jellyroll fashion. Seal edges with butter or water, pinching to seal. Cut to fit the greased pans or forms. Bake in preheated 375° F. oven for 35 minutes or until it pulls away from the sides of the pan. Remove from the oven and lay on side to cool—on baking rack—to prevent the bread from getting "heavy." Brush with a bit of butter or glaze while still slightly warm.

ORCHARD

*R*aspberry brambles, the grape arbor, and the orchard's line of apple, peach, and pear trees helped define our boundaries and our lives on the farm.

When my cousins, brother, and I were sent out to play, our "orders" often were issued in geographical terms: "Stay in the grass on this side of the grape arbor." "No climbing in the cherry trees." "Don't go beyond the apple trees."

Of course, our directions weren't all that different when we were tackling our summer chores. We heard: "Pick the raspberries from the first row of bushes," "Be sure to check under the leaves of the strawberry plants closest to the rhubarb," and "The peaches on the tree closest to the barn should be ripe."

In summer, the farm produced enough fruit to fill what we children believed was a bottomless fruit bowl. When we weren't picking vegetables, we hunted for the bright red strawberries in our patch or scoured the countryside for their smaller, but equally delicious, wild cousins. Next, we

Left: Orchard blossoms and dandelions are springtime delights in Lancaster County.

scaled ladders in the tree limbs to pluck the sour cherries, the midnight-maroon Bing cherries, and the bright yellow and red-blushed Queen Anne cherries from their branches.

Back on the ground, there were the blues of wild huckleberries in low-trailing bushes and the reds and blacks of the season's domestic and wild raspberries that were outnumbered at least 12 to 1 by the thorns on the scraggly canes.

We got to straighten up again to pick the fuzzy golden peaches, but also did plenty of bending to harvest my grandmother's pride and joy—the Persian melons—and the crop of heavy green watermelons. Grapes, dark reds and green, came next, along with the nearly opaque fruit of yellow-green Bartlett pears. The season ended on ladders, in the orchard, with apple-picking.

Although the vegetable and fruit-picking chores could get tedious, our parents tempted us with rewards. If we could each finish pitting two or three gallons of sour cherries, we could go swimming in Pequea Creek. If it was too cold to swim, we could take some time to go fishing or just play games.

The promise of rewards was vital because gathering berries or snipping a hand of grapes from the vine could be complicated and much more dangerous than pushing a shopping cart through a crowded supermarket's produce section. From the season's start to its end, we faced nature's challenges. There were changing weather patterns, invasions by battalions of natural pests, encounters with life-threatening beasts, and "rustlers" in the melon patch. But more on this later.

We children "risked" our lives to gather fruit, making our farm adventures no less thrilling than taming the Wild West.

When delicate white blossoms made the barren branches of our locust trees look like larger-than-life Oriental fans, we knew the fruit season was about to begin. The adults willing to pluck the blossoms from the thorny branches turned them into something called Dutchman's Champagne—a white, sparkling wine with ample kick. We children welcomed the sight of the trees in bloom because it was generally acknowledged that when the weather was warm enough for the blossoms to emerge, it also was warm enough for our toes to emerge from our shoes. Finally, the delicate perfume emanating from the blossoms gently awakened our resident honeybees from their long winter's rest.

Their hives, located about 10 feet from our sitting room window, were a constant reminder that we had work to do, too. We could hear them buzzing from sunrise to sunset and watch them frantically taking off and landing on blossoms of all kinds as well as the hives. Watching them for even a few minutes gave meaning to the expression "busy as a bee." Of course, we understood why they seemed a little frantic and put in such long hours when our parents told us it would take one bee 200,000 trips, from hive to flower and back to the hive, to make one pound of honey.

The light, golden honey my Uncle Emory gathered from those hives added summer's sweetness to foods, even in midwinter. The best of the honeycombs, supported by sturdy, hexagonal lattice-work of wax, were popped into jars and then surrounded with honey. Honey from the combs that weren't as pretty was strained and put into jars. For a special kid-treat, we combined honey with peanut butter,

Right: Honey-producing beehives are frequently found at the orchard's edge. Pages 108–109: Ripe, red, just-picked cherries may soon appear in a Groff recipe creation.

elevating both basic ingredients into a heavenly mixture, and spread it onto homemade bread still warm from the oven. Of course, bread spread with just honey and butter was an acceptable snack, too, particularly when we each had a mug of hot chocolate to wash down the sticky sweetness.

Occasionally, however, the adults managed to use some honey for other purposes. My aunt spooned golden honey into her morning tea. She and my mother occasionally spooned some into dishes like rhubarb crumble and sweet potatoes. It also was an accepted remedy for a bad cough. Children got a mixture of warm honey and lemon juice, while the adults kicked it up a notch by mixing the honey and lemon with dandelion wine for a Pennsylvania Dutch-style hot toddy.

First-of-the-season strawberries, fragrant and as big as our thumbs, were the embodiment of all that was good about the summer to come. They could be popped into our mouths during a quick break from playing or working. But when the crop ripened in earnest, we focused on serious and concentrated berry-eating and berry-picking. Sometimes, we raced against birds that took pecks out of the berries because they were thirsty. Other times, we raced to pick ripe berries before a stretch of rainy weather turned them sodden and spongy.

No one wanted to see any strawberries ruined or go to waste when there were so many grand ways to savor their goodness. One of the best and simplest ways to enjoy them was slicing them when they're still warm from the sun and then pouring a cool stream of sweetened milk over them. Now, that was a heavenly tonic we children could appreciate far more than the foul-tasting spring brew adults made from boiled dandelion greens.

Slightly more complicated, but no less delicious, were our fruit soups. Long before they became fashionable features on restaurant menus, we made them as light meal fare or desserts. Even better was the idea that we children could make them for ourselves or the family.

First, of course, came the stemming and cleaning of the berries. Then came the task I liked—stripping the crusts from white bread and cutting or tearing the slices into small cubes. Once the cubes were sprinkled into the bottoms of cereal-sized bowls, berries were mixed in, and sweetened milk or cream was poured in. The milk soaked into the bread and carried the fruit's flavor from cube to cube. When cherries, raspberries, and peaches were ripe and ready, they, too, became the makings of similar chilled fruit soups.

No less delicious, to some people, is the combination of strawberries and fresh rhubarb in pies and cobblers. The pinkish rhubarb stalks and sweet strawberries always were ready at the same time and grew next to each other in our garden. But was it natural and right to combine them in pies and cobblers?

It's a culinary issue that can divide families and friends. I personally like the rhubarb, *sans* its poisonous green leaves, best when it is thoroughly cooked and combined with mandarin oranges. So that it won't be stringy, only the hearts should be cut into small pieces, for pies.

I must admit, however, that others don't share my fondness for this vegetable that resembles red celery. They claim stewed rhubarb and berries, strawberry-rhubarb crumble, and strawberry-rhubarb bread were created for the same reasons carrots go into cake and zucchini goes into bread—because desperate cooks could find no other ways to get their families to eat it.

Our family wasn't divided about other berry desserts like strawberry shortcake and berries with golden sponge cake. But before the season ended in mid-June, we also enjoyed strawberries in some particularly kid-pleasing ways. They provided a dramatic, scarlet-red topping for snowy mountains of homemade vanilla ice cream. When they were sliced and combined with the cream in the hand-cranked freezer, they created ice cream that looked as if it was studded with rubies. The first taste was heavenly… The second erased all memories of stooping over in the scorching heat to pick those berries… The third was enough to make us offer to pick more berries the following day, if we could make more ice cream, too.

The only time we ventured near the sweet cherry trees on the lawn was when the fruit needed to be picked. At all other times, my mother and the birds took turns keeping a close watch on the trees. They and she knew when the fruit was ripe, and then the race began to see whether the birds would beat us to the harvest.

My mother was a formidable rival for the ornery bunch of starlings who wanted to lay claim to the fruit. When they started flying in and out of the trees too frequently to suit mother, she'd grab one of dad's shotguns. Armed for battle, she'd fire a few shots into the trees to ruffle their feathers. The rest of the time, she relied on us to make enough noise to keep the birds from enjoying too many cherries.

Finally, when the fruit was dead-ripe, she'd give the ok for us to climb the ladders and "save" the cherry crop. At first, it was pure sport to be in the trees that normally were off-limits. Breaking branches or even bumping the delicate cherry blossoms would reduce the number of big, juicy cherries we'd get. But sending my cousins, brother, and me to pick the cherries was just about as dangerous as releasing a flock of hungry birds in the tree.

One for the bucket…one for me…one for the bucket…two for me… At first, those shiny, deep-red cherries were v-e-r-y slow to pile up in our containers. Although we knew our parents wanted the cherries for special occasions, we couldn't think of a happier event to celebrate than being in those trees. We ate as much of the fruit as we could eat, before filling our buckets. Of course, the pits also were the airborne ammunition for more than a few seed-spitting contests.

When we climbed down out of the trees, the beautiful Bing and Queen Anne cherries we carried to the kitchen were either served fresh when we had guests joining us for dinner or were canned for future festive meals. Occasionally, when the sweet cherry harvest was particularly abundant, we indulged more frequently in treats like cherries and cream, cherries and juice over sponge cake, or cherries atop still-warm, oven-baked rice pudding. Also welcome was an ice cream freezer full of black cherry-vanilla ice cream.

Sour cherries weren't nearly as hard for us to resist. Just popping one into your mouth made you feel as if your lips would stay puckered for a month. Cherry, pit and all, invariably went flying if anyone happened to forget the previous season's tasting lesson.

But once the sour cherries were out of the trees, our parents had all kinds of ways to boost their taste-appeal. Heavily sugared, they could be eaten fresh. But equally rewarding were slices of bright-red sour cherry pies under crowning scoops of vanilla ice cream. Another family favorite was a treat we'd have for our evening meal—cornbread studded with cherries. I loved it, but when I first attempted to make it for my own family, I could not understand why the cherries sank to the bottom rather than simply being scattered here and there throughout the bread. When I bemoaned this fact to my mother, she realized she had forgotten to tell me to sprinkle the cherries with flour before folding them into the batter.

No matter whether we were preparing sweet or sour cherries, my father and uncle always insisted the fruit needed to be hand-pitted. They had absolutely no faith in hand-cranked cherry pitters because, they explained, no one could ever make a pitter the right size for every cherry. They had nearly broken their teeth on enough mechanically "pitted" cherries to prove their point.

Despite even careful hand-pitting, it seemed like an occasional cherry pit would slip through our hands and into the pie filling. And if there was a pit anywhere in the pie, Dad invariably found it in his piece. My husband Abe

never experienced this kind of bad luck. But late- ly, I've found enough pits in my slices of pie to wonder if Dad is having a good laugh on me.

I mentioned earlier that gathering fruit could be a life-threatening task—a point made on one of my brother's huckleberry-picking expeditions in a central Pennsylvania thicket. Huckleberries, as blue as blueberries and often better tasting, grow on low bushes in the wilds. Rattlesnakes sometimes seek cover under their branches. But that wasn't the problem Raymond encountered.

He headed for the hilltop where we always

gathered moss and ferns to turn our fishbowls into terrariums when the goldfish we'd won at summer and autumn fairs had died.

"We found loads of bushes, heavily laden with huckleberries," he said. "We picked two quarts very quickly and were figuring we'd be able to gather plenty more when we heard a large snarl from a mama bear and some baby-snorts from her cubs. They apparently wanted us to leave some berries for their lunch. But we were even more generous. They didn't have to shake the bushes for their berries. They could just enjoy the buckets of huckleberries we dropped when we ran for our lives."

Picking peaches wasn't nearly as dangerous. The worst that could happen was that we could get a little itchy from the velvety fuzz encasing each peach or be stung by a yellow jacket intent on savoring the same peach.

The cling peaches (the ones that won't release their pits without a struggle) were the first to ripen. We used them for eating out of hand, dicing into our cool fruit soups, and slicing into pies and tarts.

Next came the golden, freestone peaches that released their pits more easily. We canned as many of these as we could get from our own trees and then supplemented the harvest with more fruit we purchased from commercial orchards. Mother always bought top-quality fruit because she believed it took more time to work with damaged or small fruit. Besides, using the less desirable fruits also meant the peaches canned for winter wouldn't look as good as she wanted and that really would go against her grain. She believed that the foods we ate had to be beautiful to look at, as well as good tasting, even if that required some special techniques.

Because we had only cold running water in the farm kitchen, we boiled water in a big old tin kettle on the coal stove. Then, we poured the hot water over about 12 peaches at a time, a process that shocked the peaches into releasing their skins. We just used our fingers to pull the loosened skin off the fruit, and either cut the peaches in half or cut them into slices. The halves, in particular, had to be placed in the glass canning jars a certain way so that the red-tinged centers always faced out. Each jar also contained one peach pit, which Mother claimed enhanced the flavor. A little lemon juice was added, too, to make sure the fruit maintained its beautiful color.

Last to ripen and best of all were the white peaches with their succulently sweet fruit and pinkish centers. A few of these were eaten fresh, but most were carefully canned to be "company fruit." I remember wishing we could have the whites each time I was sent to the cold cellar for a jar of peaches, but knew better than to reach for them unless very special guests were expected for dinner.

White grapes were nearly as coveted as the white peaches. But their care began long before we snipped bunches from the vine.

We all watched and waited for all of our grapevines to blossom. Just as soon as they did, the blossoms signaled where bunches would develop. Then, armed with brown paper bags we'd been saving all year, we carefully covered the blossoms by tying the bags around them. This precaution kept the growing grapes safe from insects and from any sprays that had to be used.

White grapes were crushed for sparkling white grape juice, while the red and purple grapes were either blended with sugar and spices to begin fermenting for wine, or went into pies or jellies and jams.

Persian melons, an important cash crop for us, resembled cantaloupes, but were oh so much better. My grandmother developed the line and carefully saved the seeds from year to year for these melons that were larger than lopes and sweeter, too. Similar in color, and with the same netting pattern on the surface, they brought us customers from as far away as downtown Philadelphia. We coddled them from start to finish.

When we were sure there wouldn't be any more frosts, we carefully planted the melon seedlings we had nurtured on our windowsills. Once in the ground, they were covered with little parchment caps secured by wires to protect them from birds and other garden bandits. Their progress under the parchment was a source of amusement for us and a bit of wonderment for our Amish friends. In farm country, where there's competition to see who gets the earliest produce, we always were the first to have ripe melons. But we didn't realize how much this interested our neighbors until the day we spotted the eldest member of the Amish family furtively crossing the meadow, jumping the creek between the two homes, and then lifting the little caps to peek at the plants. He thought we planted seeds, rather than seedlings, and so couldn't figure out how our melons sprouted first.

Once the melon vines began spreading in the rich, sandy soil mounds we'd made for them near the creek, we carefully picked up the stems and wrapped them back on themselves, like styling a hairdo, so that we could pull the weeds growing under them. Then we'd carefully replace the vines in their original positions so the fruit could continue growing. Once the melons were the size of tennis balls, we just let them alone because the vines were big enough to snuff out any weeds that dared emerge.

Even picking the fruit was an art. The melons, which could grow to weigh 9 or 10 pounds, were ripe when the background behind the netting pattern was still green and the center of the melon (rather than the stem or blossom ends) gave just a little when touched with a thumb. Then it was time to cut them open, exposing a seed area no larger than a softball, and lots of luscious, orangey flesh.

Our watermelons attracted attention, too, because they were so good and so close to the road. One summer, they were just too much to resist for a crowd of local boys who were in the habit of raiding farmers' fields for good things to eat.

When my dad heard from neighboring farmers that the boys had begun making their summer rounds, he was ready for them. Just after dark, when the boys were settling in for a feast on our melons they'd just cut open, Dad turned a flashlight on. They were like a herd of stunned deer— staring back into the light.

Dad said, "Boys I'm glad you like our watermelons. I'm so glad, in fact, that I want all of you to come back here tomorrow afternoon at 4 p.m. to have some more."

The boys knew better than to ignore his invitation because Dad knew all of their parents. When they arrived the next day, he had set out at least a dozen melons and told the boys they could have all they wanted, and more. In fact, he made sure they ate and ate, until their faces were sticky and streaked with juice. They were thoroughly sick of melons before Dad sent them home to eat their dinners.

His "cure" lasted even longer than expected. No boys raided his fields again that season or in any of the ones to come. When Dad heard other farmers complain about the youthful marauders, he could just shrug since no one ever seemed to bother his melons.

Pears weren't a big crop for us. They were just another fruit adding variety to our table. Sometimes, they were poached or halved and canned. At other times, they were cooked down into pear butter.

Apples, however, figured into nearly every slice of our lives. They were on our table in some form at practically every meal. They were the makings of snacks and celebrations, sustenance and satisfaction. As the last of the summer days cooled and autumn began, the days could be as crisp as the apples we were preparing to pick.

We children knew better than to conduct our own tests to see if the apples were ripe. Our parents had warned us, "Eat green apples and we'll know it within 12 hours because you'll all have stomachaches."

We had to use our resourcefulness to figure another way to know when we could start snacking in the apple orchard. Our Amish playmates supplied the solution. All they had to do was give an apple to one of their carriage horses. If the horse willingly took the apple, chomped on it, swallowed it, and nuzzled us for more, we knew the apples were ready for us, too. However, if the horse took one bite and sent the rest of the apple flying, the fruit was still too green.

Winesaps, Smokehouse, and Jonathon

apples were family favorites for their tastes and textures. The cider, applesauce, apple butter, and apple pies made from them were flavorful to their core.

When you walk through one of our Pennsylvania German farmers' markets or stop at a roadside stand in the autumn, you're likely to find fresh cider, homemade *schnitz* (dried apple slices), and apple dumplings.

Practically every farm family had their own secret blend of apples that were combined and squeezed at the cider mill to make their special cider. Tasting the various types was fun that, I suspect, became even more of a pastime when the brews began to ferment.

Apple dumplings, more than crisps and strudels, were autumn desserts everyone appreciated. Before the apples were encased in biscuit dough, they were sprinkled with butter and brown sugar. Next, they were baked and served with warm milk.

But there were other variations, depending on the occasion. Rather than make individual dumplings for a crowd, we sometimes lined up the apples in soldierly rows in a baking pan and then covered them with a sheet of biscuit dough. For an entirely different dessert, and one that's more old-fashioned, the dumplings were wrapped in cheesecloth and plunged into boiling water. When removed from the water and dried a bit, they had the texture of an old fashioned steamed pudding.

Many of the apples we picked or bought were turned into apple *schnitz*, the Pennsylvania German forerunner of apple chips and other such dried fruit snacks. It took all of us working together to process a normal-sized batch of dried apple slices—10 bushels at a time. Once the apples were peeled and sliced, they were laid out on muslin sheets and dried slowly from the inside out till they were a caramel brown and chewy. Sometimes, they were eaten out of hand as snacks. But often, they were soaked in water or cider to reconstitute them, drained, and then baked into Amish-style half-moon pies. These snack-sized pies, often passed to children to quiet them in church, were some of the best bribes anyone could get.

Although my family didn't believe in cherry pitters, they willingly would have sold stock in the cast iron apple peelers designed and made in Mount Joy, a small town on the western side of Lancaster County where I and most of my family live today. I raced my cousins and brother for a shot at one of the two apple peelers clamped to the worktable. Although we had to stand up to crank the peeler and used it for hours on end, this was a task that turned into pure sport. Apples of similar size were chosen, loaded onto the machines and, with "ready, set, go," became the competitors in race after race.

Although there were dozens of variations on apple peelers, the devices were simple but efficient. Once the apple was impaled on a fork-like holder, turning the crank sent the blades spinning around the apple's round cheeks. When the peeler had gone from one end to another, it automatically pushed the finished apple into a waiting pan of water. The apples then were cored and sent from the outbuilding where we were working to the kitchen, where they were poured into kettles and slowly cooked down into the applesauce that was canned for winter.

Before processing the rest of the harvest into apple jelly and apple butter or even spiced apples, the adults carefully selected the best of the apples and packed them in layers in barrels

Left: When I was young, watermelon was a favorite summer treat.

of straw in the cold cellar. With a little luck and skill, too, the apples lasted long enough to be baked into holiday pies and tarts.

When autumn had arrived in earnest and we had to bundle ourselves for the cold, we turned to one of our last food preservation tasks—making apple butter. Like honey, it was always on the table and ready to be spread on bread. But it also was our forerunner to a dish like yogurt with fruit on the bottom. The only difference was that we swirled ribbons of apple butter into cottage cheese. Even today, you'll see tubs of apple butter alongside cottage cheese on salad bars in Pennsylvania Dutch country.

Apples were peeled and cored the day before we planned to make the apple butter. The next morning, a wood fire was lit to heat a big copper kettle that was filled with fresh apples, dried apple slices, and cider. The mixture, which had to cook all day long, had to be stirred constantly to prevent it from sticking to the bottom and burning. At first, it was fun to take our place at the kettle and work the paddle through the thickening mass of apples. But after a while, the novelty wore off. Slowly, ever so slowly, the apples would break down into sauce. Even more

slowly, the mixture thickened and darkened.

While it was cooking, some families added some cinnamon and spice blends to the mixture. But we preferred the taste of deep, pure apples. The only occasional additions were wisps of smoke that added a hint of flavor to the apple butter.

As it became harder and harder to move the paddle through the apple butter that had turned about as dark as chocolate cake, we hoped it soon would be time to test the butter. We children practically cheered when the adults signaled us to get a small plate from the kitchen to conduct the test. Slowly and deliberately, my mother or aunt would spoon some apple butter onto the plate. As we gathered around to watch the final test, we were as silent as spectators watching a high roller shoot for a jackpot. At last, the plate was turned upside down. Would the apple butter be so thin that it would drop off? Or would it be so thick it would stick to the plate like glue? We watched. We waited. The apple butter stayed on the plate. We were free at last!

Left: Apples await the truck pick-up in a Lancaster County orchard.

BASIC PIE DOUGH
YIELDS: TWO 9-INCH PIE SHELLS, OR ONE DOUBLE CRUST PIE.

I like to make a large quantity of these crumbs, doubling the recipe once or twice. I only use the amount I need for the day by adding the water, and refrigerate the rest in a sealed container. Usually the amount you can hold in both hands together, before adding the water, is enough for one crust. These crumbs will keep in the refrigerator for at least four weeks.

2-1/2 cups flour
1/2 cup fresh lard or vegetable shortening
1/4 cup butter (1/2 stick)
3/4 teaspoon salt
Ice water, approx. 1/3 cup

In a large bowl, combine the shortening, butter, salt, and flour with a pastry blender or rub with your hands until fine. Carefully dribble water evenly over the crumbs with one hand while tossing the crumbs lightly with the other. Use only enough water to hold together. When dough becomes moist, gently press it to the side of the bowl. The less it is handled, the flakier it will be. If you are using a food processor, add the water cautiously, watching for the moment it starts to form a ball. Divide in half. Pat the sides of each ball to prevent uneven edges before rolling. Generously flour a board or counter, making sure the top and bottom of the dough are floured. Roll the dough about 1/8-inch thick, moving the rolling pin lightly until the round crust is about an inch larger than the pie pan. Place in pie pan, cutting off any excess dough. Crimp the edges with your fingers or a pastry crimper. Keep the excess dough to the side, covering with plastic wrap. Do not use the dough over and over again or it will become dry and tough. When finished with pie pans, combine the extras, moisten with a bit of water and roll.

To par-bake shells (this prevents soggy crusts) for fruit pies or other pies that do not call for a pre-baked crust, place in preheated 350° F. oven for approx. 7 to 10 minutes or until the pastry puffs. Remove at once and gently press any bubbles that may have formed. Fill, top, and bake according to directions.

To fully bake shells, prick the dough a few times with a fork to prevent shrinkage and bake approx. 20 minutes or until dry and golden brown. Cool and store or fill with desired filling.

BASICS

Vanilla Sauce

2/3 cup sugar
3 Tablespoons flour
1/4 teaspoon salt
1-1/2 cups water
1 teaspoon vanilla extract
1/2 teaspoon lemon extract
1 Tablespoon butter

In a heavy 1-quart saucepan, add the sugar, flour, and salt. Gradually add the water, stirring to make a smooth sauce. Bring to a boil over medium heat, stirring constantly, and simmer for 2 minutes. Remove from heat and add vanilla, lemon extract, and butter. Whisk until well blended. If you prefer a thinner sauce, add a bit of hot water and stir until smooth.

Fruit with Sour Cream
SERVES 4 TO 6

4 cups fresh fruit, cut in bite–size pieces, or use all one kind of fruit such as blueberries, strawberries, etc.
8 ounces light sour cream
1/2 cup yogurt (I prefer fruited for variety)
1/3 cup light brown sugar
Several dashes grated nutmeg
Pinch of salt

Place cut fruit in large bowl. Cover with plastic wrap.

Combine the remaining ingredients in another bowl, stirring until brown sugar is dissolved. Cover with plastic wrap and refrigerate for several hours. This may be made the day before, if desired, leaving the cutting of the fruit for the time you are ready to serve it. I prefer to serve the fruit and sauce separately, letting each person pour as much sauce as desired.

This recipe is very refreshing in the summer.

FRUIT FILLING FOR PIES
FILLING FOR ONE PIE

3 Tablespoons arrowroot (if unavailable,
  use cornstarch)
$^1/_2$ cup water or fruit juice
1 cup sugar (less if desired)
1 teaspoon lemon juice
Dash of nutmeg
$^1/_4$ teaspoon salt
2-$^1/_2$ cups berries, cherries, or sliced fruit

In deep saucepan, dissolve the arrowroot in the water. Add the sugar and bring to a boil, stirring until slightly thickened. Remove from heat, stir in the lemon juice, nutmeg, salt, and berries or fruit.

Pour into par-baked pie shell (recipe on page 117) and sprinkle with a $^1/_2$-inch layer of pie crumb topping.

Bake fruit pies in a 350° F. oven for 45 minutes, or until the fruit begins to bubble along the edges. Cool a bit to enable the fruit to jell.

PEACH OR APRICOT BISQUE

SERVES 6

This refreshing fruit soup is so adaptable, you will want to try different fruits, like blueberries, strawberries, etc.

1 pound fresh fruit, peeled and pitted
6 Tablespoons light brown sugar
1 cup sour cream
1 quart half-and-half or milk
1 Tablespoon cinnamon
1 teaspoon nutmeg
3 Tablespoons brandy or 1 Tablespoon brandy flavoring
Whipped cream (see page 85) or fresh fruit for garnish (fresh mint leaves are great, too)

In a blender or food processor, puree the fruit and sugar. Add the sour cream, half-and-half, and half of the spices. Refrigerate for several hours to blend the flavors. Stir in the brandy just before serving. Sprinkle the top of each serving with remaining spices, then top with a dollop of whipped cream or sliced fruit. If you chill the bowls before filling, the soup will stay cold longer. It's also pretty to serve on crushed ice.

STRAWBERRY SHORTCAKE
SERVES 6

An All–American dessert, this recipe is great for any fresh berries. We especially enjoyed this because strawberries were the first fruits in our garden. If we didn't have time to make the cake, we would cube white bread; with the sugared berries and milk it was quite delicious.

Cake:
4 eggs, beaten
1/2 cup (scant) shortening
2 cups (scant) sugar
5 cups flour
4 teaspoons baking powder
1/2 teaspoon salt
1-3/4 cups milk

4 cups sliced strawberries
1 cup whole strawberries
1/2 cup granulated sugar
1 cup whipping cream—whipped

In mixing bowl, beat the eggs, shortening, and sugar until fluffy. Sift together the flour, baking powder, and salt. Alternate adding the milk and dry ingredients into the shortening mixture until batter is smooth. Pour into a greased 9 x 13 inch baking pan or an 11-inch Bundt pan and bake in preheated 350° F. oven for 50 minutes or until testing pin comes out clean when inserted.

To serve, cut in squares and split. Put sliced and sugared strawberries between layers, add some whipped cream and whole berries on top. Or serve in a deep dish or bowl with milk—regular or sweetened.

CORN BREAD WITH CHERRIES
YIELDS: 2 SMALL LOAVES

1-1/2 cups yellow cornmeal
1 cup all-purpose flour
1/3 cup sugar
1 teaspoon salt
1 Tablespoon baking powder
2/3 cup butter
2 eggs
1-1/2 cups milk
1 cup pitted fresh cherries coated
  with 1/3 cup flour
Use basic fruit recipe for pies on page 119

Sift cornmeal, flour, sugar, salt, and baking powder into a large bowl. In a mixing bowl, cream the butter and eggs. Combine the dry ingredients with the creamed mixture alternately with the milk. Do not over–beat. Pour into a greased 9-inch square cake pan, two loaf pans, or individual molds. Sprinkle the cherries rolled in flour on top of the dough after filling the baking pans. Press the fruit lightly into the mixture. Bake in preheated 375° F. oven for approx. 30 minutes or until a toothpick inserted in thickest part comes out clean. Cool slightly before taking out of pan. Invert on rack if you are using cast-iron molds. Top with cherry fruit filling.

APPLE OR PEACH DUMPLINGS
SERVES 6

Fruit should be cored and pitted.
Peel if desired.

6 medium baking apples or 6
   medium peaches
$\frac{1}{2}$ cup cinnamon candies or $\frac{1}{2}$ cup
   granulated sugar and 1 teaspoon
   cinnamon and $\frac{1}{8}$ teaspoon nutmeg
2 cups flour
2-$\frac{1}{2}$ teaspoons baking powder
$\frac{1}{2}$ teaspoon salt
1 cup butter—$\frac{2}{3}$ cup in dough, $\frac{1}{3}$ in syrup
$\frac{1}{2}$ cup milk
Flour for rolling dough
2 cups light brown sugar
2 cups water
$\frac{1}{8}$ teaspoon cinnamon
$\frac{1}{3}$ cup butter

In a small bowl, combine the sugar mixture, if using. Fill the center of each apple with cinnamon candies or sugar mixture. If using peaches, the sugar mixture is best. Set aside until dough is ready.

In large bowl, sift the flour, baking powder, and salt together. Cut in $\frac{2}{3}$ cup butter with pastry cutter or by hand until fine and crumbly. Sprinkle the milk over the crumbs until moist, pressing into a ball. Do not overwork the dough. Divide dough into as many parts as you have fruit. Pat the edges to make a nice even pastry. Generously flour the pastry board and the top of each pastry. Roll thin enough to cover the fruit.

Place the fruit in center of dough, wrapping dough so fruit is completely covered. If you prefer to have the fruit showing, leave the center open, sealing by crimping the edges.

Moisten the edges with water to fasten securely. Place dumplings 1 inch apart in greased 9-by13-inch baking dish or pan.

Combine brown sugar, water, and spice in saucepan. Bring to a boil, stir and simmer for 3 to 5 minutes. Remove from heat and stir in the $\frac{1}{3}$ cup butter. When melted, pour syrup over dumplings. Bake in preheated 350° F. oven for 35 to 40 minutes, basting with syrup every 15 minutes. Serve hot with chilled milk, cream, ice cream, or whipped cream. Serve as an appetizer, main course, or dessert.

HONEY APPLE CRISP
SERVES 6

6 to 8 baking apples, cored, peeled
  and sliced
2 Tablespoons lemon juice
$1/2$ cup water
$3/4$ cup flour
$1/2$ cup cup dry oatmeal
$3/4$ cup light brown sugar
$1/3$ cup butter or margarine
$1/3$ teaspoon cinnamon
$1/2$ teaspoon salt
Dash each of cloves, ginger, and nutmeg
$1/4$ cup honey

Combine the lemon juice and water in large bowl. Toss the sliced apples in the liquid until completely coated. Pour into buttered 2-quart baking dish. Combine flour, oatmeal, brown sugar, butter or margarine, cinnamon, salt, and spices. Cut with pastry cutter or by hand to make fine crumbs.

Spread the crumbs evenly over apples. Dribble the honey over the top and bake uncovered in preheated 375° F. oven for approx. 40 minutes, or until it bubbles around the sides. Serve warm with milk, cream, whipped cream, or ice cream.

APPLE BUTTER
YIELDS: 3-1/2 QUARTS

12 pounds cooking apples (not Delicious apples; try Winesap, Smokehouse, or Jonathan)
2 cups water
3-1/2 cups granulated sugar
1 cup cider vinegar
1/2 teaspoon salt
1/2 teaspoon cinnamon

Wash, core, peel, and quarter the apples. Place the apples and water in a large pot. Cover, bring to a boil, reduce heat to low, and simmer until the apples are soft, approx. 20 minutes. Run through food mill, sieve, or blend in food processor. Return the sauce to the pot and stir in the sugar, vinegar, salt, and cinnamon, mixing well. Pour mixture into a heavy roaster pan and bake uncovered in a preheated 375° F. oven for approx. 2-1/2 hours. Stir every 15 minutes with a wooden spoon to prevent burning around the sides. If it starts to get very brown around the edges, reduce the heat to 350° F. Be sure to blend well during stirring to ensure an even color when finished.

The apple butter is ready to jar or freeze when you can place 2 Tablespoons of it on a saucer and turn it upside down without it dropping off. Ladle into hot sterilized jars and seal with new lids and rings, or cool and ladle into clean freezer containers. It will keep for several weeks.

Pear Butter

Substitute pears for apples and add 1 teaspoon nutmeg.

APPLESAUCE
YIELDS: 3 TO 4 CUPS

4 pound apples—Jonathan, Winesap, Smokehouse, Stayman, etc. (Granny Smiths are tart and may need more sugar.)
2 cups water
1-1/2 cups sugar—less if desired
Pinch of salt

Wash, core, peel, and quarter the apples. Place water in large saucepan, add the apples and bring to a boil. Cover and simmer on low until the apples are soft, approx. 15 minutes. Remove from heat and press through food mill or sieve. If you prefer a chunky sauce, use a food processor or hand masher. Place sauce back in pan and stir in the sugar and salt. Check for sweetness, adding more if desired. On low heat, bring to a boil, stirring for about 5 minutes. Serve warm with a dash of cinnamon or Spiced Whipped Cream (see page 90).

This freezes well after being properly cooled.

FUN FOOD

*hese days, there aren't many foods you can't buy. Sticky buns as big as bricks, buttery caramel corn by the bucketful, and soft pretzels in fancy flavors are as close at hand as your nearest shopping mall.

Trouble is that no matter how much you pay for these treats, they aren't packaged with the memories that come from making them at home with your children and grandchildren.

I'll never forget the wonderful times I spent in the kitchen with my mother, aunt, and grandmother, and I've tried to pass some of those experiences along to my own family and now to you.

Our two sons were in the kitchen with me from the time they could bang a wooden spoon on a pot, and they never left. John, the youngest, loved tackling kitchen projects on his own. When he was old enough, he'd take command of the stove after a successful fishing expedition and make a grilled trout dinner for all of us. Or, he'd prepare a batch of cooking clay to encase and bake Cornish hens for an incredible feast. His older brother, Charlie, loved cooking so much that he graduated from the Culinary Institute of America and today runs the kitchens and restau-

Left: Lancaster's Amish youth ice skate on a farm pond.

rants at Groff's Farm and Golf Course. But your children don't have to want to become professional chefs to enjoy cooking with you.

In my own kitchen, I've continued working with my grandchildren and other children I've taken "under my wing." The results have been as rewarding as a warm loaf of lemon-glazed raisin bread and as much fun as making ice cream the old-fashioned way. Observed one of the children attending a kitchen session, "Cooking is part chemistry, part math, and part fun. But the best part is that you get to eat the experiment, and there's never a problem that can't be solved."

I can't encourage you enough to do the same with your own children. I know it's hard to find time to even prepare the family's weeknight meals, but make the effort on the weekend. Search for some "found" time, that is, time you can take from something else. Cutting out as little as one TV show will provide enough time to lure children into the kitchen to make some fun food, whether it is something sweet or something hearty.

When I was growing up, my mother never forced me to cook. She made the kitchen so inviting I couldn't stay out of it. The fun she and my aunt had while they worked was part of the appeal and so were the aromas and tastes that emanated from the stove. I'd stop by to see what was going on. My mother would tell me about the food she was making, whether it was butter mints for a party or homemade noodles for someone's birthday dinner of chicken pot pie. And then she'd carefully choose a segment of the work and say, offhandedly, "The celery needs to be chopped," or "It's time to knead and shape this dough. You may do it if you'd like to." She had me, like the dough, in the palm of her hand and was helping to shape the rest of my life.

If there's one time parents are most likely to welcome children into the kitchen, it's during the holidays when there are cut-out cookies to be made and decorated. But cooking sessions with the children need to be year-round rather than during just one season of the year.

For our family, each season had its special or fun foods. Funnel cakes, for example, might be popular treats at summer carnivals and fairs, but our family was most likely to make them during cool months from autumn through spring. As we maneuvered the funnel full of batter over the frying pan, the challenge was making the most concentric rings in the pan. When the completed, plate-sized funnel cake was golden and crisp, it could be sprinkled with powdered sugar or topped with something more elaborate like some sweetened and thickened fruit filling. In my own kitchen, I've also experimented with adding some finely grated chocolate to the batter to please chocoholics in the crowd.

After a day spent ice-skating or sledding, we opened the door to mugs full of piping hot chocolate and homemade marshmallows coated with toasted coconut. Sometimes, we added some action to a quiet winter evening by popping fresh popcorn on the stove and then turning it into buttery, brown caramel corn. We usually ate it as soon as it was cool enough to handle, because it quickly became soggy. When I finally realized baking the caramel corn in the oven meant it could be made and saved, not everyone in the family was thrilled with my discovery. After all, they no longer had an excuse to eat all of it right away.

On a hot summer day, the best treat (other than ice cream) was a bucket of freshly squeezed, icy homemade lemonade served with a plate of sugar cookies. It was a standard refreshment we delivered to the field hands at least twice a day during threshing season. Because we children were told we could have the lemonade and cookies the men didn't eat, we kept a close eye on the food and made sure we collected it while there were some leftovers.

During the holidays, mother and I sometimes made hand-dipped chocolates to give as gifts, but we also tackled some easier projects, like making hollow popcorn balls that could be

filled with treats or mixing up some fudge or even some easy butter mints that could be molded into festive shapes.

Certain kinds of days also inspired my mother to make special treats. On a gray Saturday morning, when I was home to help, we'd often make a huge batch of fluffy and light, yeast-raised doughnuts. As soon as they were golden brown and coated with powdered sugar, the still-warm doughnuts were put in a napkin-lined basket that I quickly delivered to the farm and butcher shop where my dad, uncle, and the hired hands were working.

Another family I know can't get through a snowstorm without making a batch of fresh cinnamon sticky buns. All it takes is the prediction of a major storm to send them out for the ingredients they'll need. When the flakes begin falling, the dough is started and begins rising. While the mixture of corn syrup, butter, and brown sugar for the sticky topping heats on the stove, parents and children knead the dough, roll it into a rectangle, spread it with butter, and add a heavy sprinkling of cinnamon and sugar before rolling it up and cutting it into rounds

that will bake after being placed in pools of buttery goo in baking pans. They're guaranteed to be sticky from ear to ear when they sit down to share a plate of the freshly baked buns. Sometimes, if they've made an especially large batch, they'll even trudge through the snow to share a plate or two of cinnamon rolls with neighbors. If you ask me, it's a grand way to celebrate being home with nothing to do but enjoy each other's company and savor some good, hearty home-cooked food.

If I had to pick one project to try with your children, I'd suggest making homemade noodles, which are the Pennsylvania Dutch equivalent of preparing fresh pasta. Everything can be done by hand, the basic ingredients cost next to nothing, the dough is ready in a matter of minutes and rests for just half an hour before it's ready to be rolled out and cut into noodles. In addition, the taste and texture of fresh noodles enhance any meal. Convinced? I hope so.

My children and grandchildren all have loved making noodles. Here in Lancaster County, some of the most commonly made ones are cut into small squares and added to Pennsylvania Dutch chicken pot pie, which isn't a pot pie at all, but a wonderful chicken stew brimming with chewy, handmade noodles.

But all kinds of flavors and shapes are possible. I've made spinach noodles and saffron noodles. I've made thin, medium, and broad egg noodles. I've run the noodle dough through my pasta machine as a cross-cultural experiment that yielded noodles as long as strands of spaghetti. I've also let children use their imagination to hand-cut noodles in all kinds of crazy shapes. As one of my young "chefs" remarked, "It's the first time I've ever been encouraged to play with my food."

Above: In my kitchen, I'm helping Monica Herr and her mother, Lydia Herr, make pot pie dough.

BASIC SWEET DOUGH

YIELDS: 1 COFFEE CAKE OR LARGE PAN OF ROLLS

3/4 cup lukewarm milk
1/2 cup sugar
1 teaspoon salt
2 packages dry granular yeast
1/2 cup lukewarm water
Pinch of sugar
2 eggs, lightly beaten
1/4 cup butter
1/4 cup margarine
5 cups sifted flour

In a large bowl, place the milk, sugar, and salt. Stir until dissolved. In a small bowl or measuring cup, add the yeast to the lukewarm water and proof by adding a pinch of sugar. Let stand for a few minutes. If the yeast rises, it is working and ready for baking. Stir and add to the milk mixture. Add the eggs and the butter and margarine.

Gradually add the flour, using only enough to make it easy to handle. You may need more or less flour, depending on the brand of flour you're using and the amount of humidity in the air. If using an electric mixer with kneading hook, knead for approx. 4 minutes or until smooth and elastic. If dough sticks to the board or surface, lightly flour and place in greased or oiled bowl. Turn the dough until all sides are lightly covered with oil—this prevents dough from drying out. Cover with a clean damp cloth. Let rise in a draft-free area until double in size, approx. 1 hour. Knead for a minute to work out all the air bubbles. Cover again for approx. 30 minutes until almost double. Shape as desired and bake according to directions for sweet dough treats on pages 132 and 135.

STICKY BUNS

Everyone has their own preference for size.

Basic Sweet Dough (recipe on page 131)
3 Tablespoons soft butter
$^1/_2$ cup granulated sugar
1 teaspoon cinnamon
$^1/_2$ cup raisins
$^1/_2$ cup melted butter
$^3/_4$ cup light brown sugar
$^1/_2$ cup chopped nuts—pecans,
    walnuts, etc.

Follow directions for the Basic Sweet Dough recipe on page 131. After the second rising of the dough, roll it on a lightly floured board into an oblong shape. Spread the butter evenly over the dough. Mix the sugar and cinnamon together and sprinkle evenly over the dough. Sprinkle with raisins. Roll up tightly, then pinch the edges together to secure the filling. Using a sharp buttered knife, cut the roll into 1-inch slices. Pour melted butter, brown sugar, and nuts into buttered baking pans (2 9-inch rounds or 1 large baking pan). Place the slices in the butter-sugar mixture. Set in a warm place and allow to rise for 30 minutes. Bake in preheated 375° F. oven for 30 minutes, or until well-baked. Remove from oven and turn upside down on a serving dish to let the sugar-butter mixture run around the rolls. Leave pan on top of rolls for at least 3 minutes before removing. Serve warm or at room temperature.

EGG NOODLES
YIELDS: ENOUGH FOR 4

2 cups flour
1/2 teaspoon salt
4 egg yolks or 3 whole eggs
1/4 cup cold water
Extra flour for rolling, could be a cup
  or less

Put flour and salt in large mixing bowl. Make a well in the center and add the egg yolks or yokes and whites and water. Stir until well blended. A food processor or mixer with strong paddle does this very quickly. As soon as it forms a ball, knead it to make a smooth ball. Cover with plastic wrap and let stand for at least 30 minutes. If using a pasta machine, cut dough according to directions (I use a hand–operated one that makes this look like magic). If rolling by hand, divide dough in thirds. Dust a generous amount of flour on top and bottom of each piece and flour the counter, board, or pastry cloth before rolling. Roll as thin as you like—the noodles will double in thickness when cooked—trim the edges to make a neat roll and lightly flour the top. Starting at one end, roll the dough into a very tight roll, as for a jellyroll or fruit rollup. Use a sharp butcher knife, cutting the noodles into thin slices (I like 1/4 inch). As the slices fall, make sure there is enough flour to toss them lightly—do not let them stick together. Separate the noodles, place on noodle rack, clean linen towels, or tablecloth to dry a bit before cooking.

Noodles must be thoroughly dry before storing in an airtight container. If freezing, be sure there is enough flour to keep them from sticking together.

SPINACH NOODLES

For color, flavor, and variation, these are perfect.

3 cups flour
1 teaspoon salt
5 egg yolks

1 cup finely chopped fresh spinach or
  1/2 cup thawed frozen spinach, drained
1/4 cup cold water
Extra amount of flour for rolling, etc.

Follow the directions for egg noodles above and add the spinach with the eggs.

POT PIE SQUARES

Pennsylvania Dutch Pot Pie is not a baked pie, but a rich broth with noodle-type squares of dough, rolled thin like noodles, boiled with deboned meat, thinly sliced potatoes, chopped celery, parsley, and onion. This one-dish meal is so versatile, heart warming, and practical, you will want to make it often using your favorites. Vegetarians love this recipe because they can combine so many things, using a good vegetable stock. Add to any chowder or soup to make an extraordinary dish. These are similar to German Spaetzle, but easier to make.

Recipe on page 42

RIVELS

1 large egg
About ¹/₂ cup milk
¹/₂ teaspoon salt
About ³/₄ cup flour

You may wonder why the "abouts." Weather plays a part in the texture of dough, etc. If the climate is dry you will need more liquid. The moisture in the air helps control the consistency of the product.

Combine ingredients and with your fingers roll pieces of dough no larger than your thumbnail. Drop into boiling soup.

SPAETZLE

YIELDS: 3 CUPS

These are a good substitute for potatoes if sautéed in butter and browned until golden. I like a bit of saffron in the buttered water while boiling. Light and airy, they are delightful and delicious. Combine ingredients and with your fingers roll pieces of dough no larger than your thumbnail.

1-¹/₂ cups flour
³/₄ teaspoon salt
Dash of nutmeg
2 large eggs, lightly beaten
¹/₂ cup milk
8 cups water plus 1 Tablespoon butter or olive oil to prevent sticking.

Combine flour, salt, and nutmeg in a mixing bowl. Stir in the beaten eggs and gradually add milk. Beat until smooth. Force the dough through the holes of a colander or use a Spaetzle maker. In a large pot, bring the water to a rapid boil, add the butter or oil, and drop in the dough, a few at a time so they do not stick together. Boil until they rise to the surface, about 2 to 3 minutes. Reduce heat to low and simmer for 10 to 12 minutes, depending on the thickness, or as soon as they are tender and thoroughly cooked. Remove with a slotted spoon and drain. Serve as a side dish, or base for vegetables and meats.

RAISED DOUGHNUTS
YIELDS: 3 DOZEN

Basic Sweet Dough (recipe on page 131)
Approx. 3 cups vegetable or corn oil
  for frying
1/2 cup confectioners' or granulated sugar

After the second rising, knead, and roll out the dough 1/3 inch thick on a well-floured board. Cut with floured 1/3-inch doughnut cutter. Let them rise uncovered until almost doubled, approx. 40 minutes. Heat oil in a deep, heavy skillet or pan to 375° F. Gently place the doughnuts in the oil, making sure they do not touch one another. Turn them when golden brown on one side, and fry until evenly brown on each side, approx. 3 minutes. Drain on paper towels. When cooled, place the sugar in a bag and shake a few at a time until covered.

CITRUS ICE
SERVES 6

1 cup orange juice, including 1 teaspoon
  of zest of orange rind
1/4 cup lemon juice, including 1 to 2 teaspoons
  of zest of lemon rind
Grated zest and juice from 1 lime (optional)
2 cups lemon soda
2 cups grapefruit soda or Tom Collins mix
Dash or two of grated nutmeg
Garnish with thin slices of orange, lemon,
  and lime

Blend all the ingredients and pour into ice cube trays, ice rings, or regular cake pans. Freeze until firm. Serve in sherbet glasses.

This is great for a refreshing treat outdoors.

FUNNEL CAKES

YIELDS: 6 LARGE FUNNEL CAKES

These quick treats have become popular, I'm sure, because they can be made quickly and the cost is very little. Popular at county and state fairs, they seem to satisfy everyone.

1 cup flour
2 teaspoons sugar
1 teaspoon baking powder
$^1/_2$ teaspoon salt
1 large egg, lightly beaten
$^3/_4$ cup milk
Oil for frying
Confectioners' sugar, honey, maple syrup, or chocolate syrup for topping.

In a large bowl, combine the flour, sugar, baking powder, and salt. Gradually add the egg and milk until well blended. Let stand for 15 minutes. In deep skillet, add oil (about $^1/_3$ inch deep) and heat to 390° F. When oil is hot, pour the batter into a funnel, drizzling a thin stream of batter into the hot oil. One finger placed under the funnel's narrow end should control the flow of the batter, the other hand holding the broad part of the funnel. Be wise by using a mitt to hold the funnel and be careful not to burn the hand controlling the flow. Start in the center of the skillet, circling continuously until pan is filled or the desired size is reached. As soon as the cake turns golden, turn and fry until golden on the other side. Drain on paper towels. Serve hot with powdered sugar or other toppings.

You may add $^1/_4$ cup tiny chocolate chips to the batter, but it will splatter a bit. Most folks think the effort is worth it.

Soft Sugar Cookies

Yields: about 3 dozen 2-inch cookies or 1 dozen large cookies

1/2 cup butter
2 Tablespoons margarine
1-1/3 cups sugar
2 large eggs
3/4 cup buttermilk
1 teaspoon baking soda dissolved in 1
   Tablespoon hot water
1 teaspoon vanilla extract
3 cups flour
1 teaspoon baking powder
1/2 teaspoon ground nutmeg
1/4 teaspoon salt
1/4 cup raisins
Sugar for topping, if desired
Flour for testing

In large mixing bowl, cream butter, margarine, and sugar until light and fluffy. Beat in the eggs, one at a time, beating lightly. Add buttermilk, dissolved baking soda, and vanilla, mixing thoroughly. In large bowl, sift together the flour, baking powder, nutmeg, and salt. Gradually add to the creamed mixture and beat until blended. Refrigerate dough for 30 minutes or more. Preheat oven to 350° F. Test-bake only one at first; if it is too thin, add a bit more flour to the dough. Drop dough by teaspoonfuls onto a greased baking sheet, spacing them at least 2 inches apart; the size depends on you. Place raisins on top of each (we either put one in the middle or make happy faces), sprinkle with sugar, and bake for approx. 15 minutes or until light and golden. When you touch top of cookie it should bounce back. Do not overbake.

If any were left overnight, we enjoyed them with hot chocolate or coffee the next morning. Some family members liked to spread a bit of honey on the cookies and dunk them.

CARAMEL CORN

YIELDS OVER 14 CUPS

If you love popcorn as I do, try this. We are so fortunate to have Pennsylvania's largest producer of popping corn, Reist Seed Company, here in our town of Mount Joy. I can jog or walk to the plant to buy the best product in the nation, while you enjoy it in theaters and parks, and can get it in the grocery.

1 cup granulated sugar
$^1/_4$ cup lightly packed light brown sugar
6 Tablespoons light corn syrup (I use Karo)
1-$^1/_2$ teaspoons cider vinegar
6 Tablespoons water
$^1/_2$ teaspoon salt
2 Tablespoons ($^1/_4$ stick) butter
$^1/_2$ teaspoon baking soda
$^1/_2$ teaspoon vanilla extract
1 cup salted or dry roasted peanuts (optional)
14 cups popped corn (unpopped kernels removed)

Combine the sugars, syrup, vinegar, and water in large, heavy saucepan. Bring to a boil and cook over medium heat, brushing the sides of the pan with a wet pastry brush, until syrup reaches 290° F. on a candy thermometer (soft crack stage), about 12 minutes. If you do not have a thermometer, drop a bit of syrup into a glass of cold water. It should turn hard and crack into pieces when removed. Stir in the salt and cook over medium-high heat until it reaches the hard crack stage or 300° F. on the thermometer, about 3 minutes. If you do not have a thermometer, drop a few drops into more ice water; it should turn brittle at once. Remove from the heat and stir in the butter, baking soda, and vanilla until well blended. Add the nuts to the popcorn, if desired, and spread the popcorn evenly in two buttered 9 by 13 inch baking pans. Pour the syrup over all the popcorn and mix until all the kernels are coated. Bake in preheated 200° F. oven for 1 hour, stirring every 15 minutes. Cool on sheets of wax paper and store in airtight containers.

SOFT PRETZELS

Homemade pretzels are a real labor of love and also a great excuse for a party. The more people twisting, the more fun for everyone. There are many legends surrounding this treat, but I prefer the one that claims they were a monk's gift to children for learning their prayers. Best when taken right from the oven, they should be warm when served. Salted or unsalted, lots of folks like mustard or a cheese spread for dipping. I like mine lightly salted and plain.

1/2 cup warm water (105° F. to 115° F.)
1 package dry yeast
1 cup milk
1/4 cup honey or granulated sugar
4 Tablespoons (1/2 stick) butter or vegetable shortening, at room temperature
1 large egg, separated
1 teaspoon salt
4-1/2 to 5 cups flour
8 cups water
8 Tablespoons baking soda
1/4 cup coarse salt (optional)

Place warm water in a small bowl and add the yeast. Let stand for about 10 minutes until it foams. Stir until dissolved and pour into a large mixing bowl. Add the milk, honey, butter, egg yolk, and salt. Slowly add the flour until the dough is stiff enough to knead. Place on a floured surface and knead by pressing the heel of your hand into the dough and rolling the dough over again and again for about 5 minutes. Cover with a towel and let the dough rise on the board for one hour. Pinch off dough the size of golf balls. Roll with the palms of your hands into strips about 18 inches long and 1/2 inch thick. Twist each into a shape and place on a tray.

Preheat the oven to 425° F. Bring the water and baking soda to a boil in a large stainless steel saucepan or kettle (the baking soda will stain an aluminum pan) over high heat. Drop three pretzels at a time into the boiling water, making sure they do not touch each other, boiling for about 1 minute over high heat—be careful, they will become soggy if overcooked. Remove the pretzels with a slotted spoon and place them on greased cookie sheets.

When all are cooked, lightly beat the egg white and 1 Tablespoon water together with a fork. With a pastry brush, cover the top of each pretzel with the egg white mixture. Sprinkle with a small amount of coarse salt, if desired, and bake for 13 to 15 minutes or until golden brown. Remove from the oven and cool slightly on baking racks or linen towels. For reheating, tent with foil and warm in a low oven until ready to serve. If freezing them, do not add all the salt until warming them in the oven.

My husband Abe and many friends encouraged me to write a new cookbook, and I have them plus many new friends to thank for their contributions. Diane Stoneback spent countless hours listening to me spin my multi-layered stories, and then made sense of them with her fine pen. She has a special talent to draw from the inner heart. Diane, Alice Harmony, and publisher/photographer Blair Seitz sat with me to organize the book. Blair and his assistant, Angela Yarbrough, made 12 trips to my studio kitchen to create the beautiful photographs. Thank you, Blair, for your outdoor photos, which express dedication to the God-given nature we are blessed with every day. Those friends who came to my Bed and Breakfast on several evenings to taste new recipes offered support and encouragement. My editor, John Hope, put finishing touches on the words as well as weaving in edits by Laura Garger, a copy editor for the *Morning Call*, Allentown, PA. My friend Steve Rheinhold helped me with my computer; and art director Cheryl Klinginsmith embellished it all with her exciting layout. My sincere thanks to all.

Betty Groff

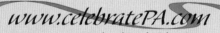